New Jersey Goes to War

*Biographies of 150 New Jerseyans
Caught Up in the Struggle of the Civil War,
including Soldiers, Civilians, Men, Women,
Heroes, Scoundrels – and a Heroic Horse*

New Jersey Goes to War

Biographies of 150 New Jerseyans Caught Up in the Struggle of the Civil War, including Soldiers, Civilians, Men, Women, Heroes, Scoundrels – and a Heroic Horse

Edited by
Joseph G. Bilby

An Official Publication of the New Jersey Civil War
Heritage Association Sesquicentennial Committee.

Printed by Longstreet House
PO Box 730, Hightstown, NJ 08520
www.Longstreethouse.com

Published by New Jersey Civil War Heritage Association
PO Box 442
Wood-Ridge, NJ 07075-0442
http://www.njcivilwar.org

ISBN 978-0-944413-75-3

Introduction by John Zinn

New Jersey is fortunate to have an active Civil War community of re-enactors, roundtables, the New Jersey Civil War Heritage Association, Sons of Union Veterans, historians, state officials and many others. In the fall of 2008, representatives of these different groups came together to discuss plans for observing the 150th anniversary of this watershed event in our state and our nation's history. The group ultimately decided to form the New Jersey Civil War 150th Anniversary Committee, an all-volunteer, not-for-profit committee that functions under the auspices of the New Jersey Civil War Heritage Association. In early December, Governor Corzine endorsed the committee's work and called on governmental agencies, not-for-profit groups and educational institutions to work with the committee.

An underlying premise of the committee's work is the belief that the Civil War era was one of the great turning points in our nation's history and that the men and women of New Jersey played an important part in those events. Unfortunately, that story has not been well understood by subsequent generations. We believe the 150th anniversary is an opportunity for increased awareness and accurate recognition of the sacrifices and contributions of the people of New Jersey during this defining time in American history. The committee will work to this end through a wide range of projects aimed towards making a lasting contribution to this effort.

This volume of biographies of 150 New Jerseyans from the Civil War era is one of our first projects. We hope that their stories will help current and future generations to get a sense of our state's involvement in those events and create excitement to learn more. On behalf of the committee I want to thank those who suggested subjects for biographies as well as to the authors who researched and wrote them. Special thanks to Joe Bilby for serving as editor, Henry F. Ballone for layout and design, and Tom Burke, John Kuhl and Jim Madden for assembling the pictures to accompany the biographies, and Dr. David Martin and Steven Glazer for their copyediting. This project has been completed in an incredibly short time frame, which testifies to this generation's desire to honor those brave women and men who made such important contributions to our state's role in the Civil War.

John G. Zinn
Chairman

Editor's Note

In commemoration of the Sesquicentennial of the Civil War, the New Jersey Civil War 150th Anniversary Committee has compiled brief biographies of 150 New Jerseyans of the era, famous and obscure, whose lives were affected by the conflict and the events surrounding it. A representative sampling, these are the stories of soldiers and civilians, including heroes, scoundrels and ordinary folks just getting by. They are men and women of diverse races, religions and ethnic backgrounds – as well as one non-human. The selections include enlisted men, officers, nurses, politicians, diplomats, manufacturers, merchants, writers, poets and artists who were born in or immigrated to our state and lived here before, during or after the war. When faced with the most climactic event in American history, the people of New Jersey's Civil War generation became, whether they wished it or not, actors upon the historical stage rather than observers. Many of their lives were, indisputably, in the oft-quoted words of Oliver Wendell Holmes, graphically "touched with fire," others less so, but all of them, for better or worse, would never be the same.

The following biographies have been submitted by a number of contributors, whose names are noted following each entry. Where applicable, sources for further information on an individual subject are noted in parentheses. Fuller citations are available in a brief selected bibliography of books, articles and manuscripts which will, in turn, often lead the reader to further sources. Internet citations provide complete access information.

Joseph G. Bilby, Editor

October, 2009

Biographies of 150 New Jerseyans Caught Up in the Struggle of the Civil War

The New Jersey Civil War 150th Anniversary Committee gratefully acknowledges the financial support of the following:

Henry F. Ballone
Peter P. Bahuk, Jr.
Joseph Bilby
Dennis Burke
Cranford (NJ) Historical Society
Gary DeSiver
Bruce Form
Genealogical Society of New Jersey
Robert Gerber
Michael and Melissa Giancarlo
Phil Kearny Civil War Round Table
Steven Glazer
John J. Hallanan
Valerie Josephson
James M. Madden
David Martin
Eleanor Silverman
John F. Swift
Joseph Truglio
Billy Van Zandt
John Zinn

Solomon Andrews was born in Perth Amboy in 1806. A physician and inventor, Andrews served as long-time mayor and public health officer of his native city. In 1849 he converted a pre-Revolutionary War barracks to house "The Inventor's Institute," where he invented and produced a wide variety of useful products, including a burglarproof lock. Andrews made significant improvements to Perth Amboy's quality of life, including designing the city's first sewer system, which dramatically reduced its yellow fever toll. With the outbreak of the Civil War, he volunteered his services to the U.S. Sanitary Commission, a predecessor of the Red Cross, and accompanied Union forces during the Peninsula Campaign of 1862.

Solomon Andrews
(Wickimedia Commons)

Andrews' greatest invention grew out of his lifelong obsession with manned flight, an interest spurred by the war. He developed a vehicle that could be self-propelled and steered through the air, even into the wind, using a ship-like rudder and harnessing the forces of gravity through mechanically contracting and expanding hydrogen gas-filled, cigar-shaped bags. The doctor offered his invention to the government, promising in a letter to President Lincoln to "sail the airship…5 to 10 miles into Secessia and back again."

The "Aereon" measured 80 feet long and 20 feet wide. With Andrews at the controls, learning to fly as he went along, it first took to the sky over Perth Amboy on June 1, 1863. Despite some developmental setbacks, Andrews' theories seemed to work. Though it may well have proved useful for military purposes, the airship was so far ahead of its time that the inventor's letters to Lincoln, Secretary of War Edwin Stanton and members of Congress went unanswered. No doubt many thought him a crank.

Andrews' Aereon (Wickimedia Commons)

Actually, Andrews was closer to genius than crank. At war's end he formed the Aerial Navigation Company to advance his idea that passengers and mail could travel by air, and on June 6, 1866, flew his machine from Perth Amboy and over New York City on the way to Oyster Bay, Long Island. When he cruised above Broadway at 1,500 feet, "the commotion along that great thoroughfare was tremendous." Unfortunately, a bank failure ruined Aerial Navigation. Solomon Andrews died in Perth Amboy on October 19, 1872, ending the career of a brilliant, patriotic and far-seeing Jerseyman who always thought "outside the box." (McPhee, *Deltoid Pumpkin*; Miers, *Where the Raritan Flows*; Miers, *New Jersey and the Civil War*)

John W. Kuhl

Myer Jacob Asch was born in Philadelphia, Pennsylvania, on October 24, 1831, the eldest of eleven children of Joseph and Clarissa Ulman Asch, and was raised in his family's traditional Jewish household. Initially educated in Philadelphia, Asch attended the University of Pennsylvania for a short time and then studied dentistry in Paris, where he developed his natural ability for languages.

At the outbreak of the Civil War, Asch returned to Philadelphia. In September 1861, he traveled to Trenton and enlisted as a second lieutenant in Company H of "Halsted's Horse," a privately raised regiment that eventually became the 1ˢᵗ New Jersey Cavalry. Quickly promoted to first lieutenant, in March 1862 Asch became captain of Company H when the regiment was reorganized by Colonel **Percy Wyndham**.

Myer Jacob Asch (Bruce Form)

In the summer of 1862, Captain Asch was appointed to General John Pope's staff. When Pope was relieved after Second Bull Run, Asch traveled west with him and became chief of cavalry in the Department of the Northwest. On March 9, 1864, he was ordered back east for duty at the Cavalry Bureau in Washington, where he ordered and inspected horses for cavalry purchase. In April 1864, Captain Asch was appointed assistant adjutant general on General Augustus Kautz's staff, and on October 7, 1864, was captured by Confederates while leading a reconnaissance patrol on the Darbytown Road. After a night in Libby Prison, Asch was transferred to the Confederate prison in Danville, Virginia, where he remained until paroled on February 22, 1865. Unable to perform duty, he was mustered out of the army on March 25, 1865, and brevetted major for his service.

A civilian again, Asch returned to Philadelphia and joined Grand Army of the Republic (GAR) Meade Post #1, as well as the Military Order of the Loyal Legion. He served as secretary to the Executive Committee and assistant to the Director General of the Philadelphia Centennial Exposition in 1876. Asch's work with foreign exhibitors during the Exposition won him decorations and honorary knighthoods from a number of European governments.

Myer Asch moved to New York City in 1878, where he worked in a family business and remained active in veterans' organizations. Major Asch died on February 16, 1890, as a result of complications from surgery for kidney ailments attributed to his confinement in Danville. He was buried in Cypress Hills Cemetery in Brooklyn. (Longacre, *Jersey Cavaliers*; *NY Times* Obituary)

Bruce M. Form

2

George Ashby was born in Burlington, New Jersey, on January 25, 1844. In 1864, Ashby, an African-American then living in Crosswicks, enlisted as a private in the 45th United States Colored Infantry, organized at Camp William Penn outside of Philadelphia between June and August of 1864. He served in Virginia during the siege of Petersburg and was present for the Confederate surrender at Appomattox Court House in April 1865. At the end of hostilities, the 45th, with a large number of other federal troops, was transferred to Texas on occupation duty. While serving with his regiment, Ashby was promoted several times until he reached the rank of first sergeant of Company H.

The flag of Sergeant Ashby's regiment, designed by David Bustill Bowser. (Library of Congress)

Sergeant Ashby was mustered out of the service at Philadelphia with the 45th in November 1865 and returned to his life as a New Jersey small farmer. After the war, he married Phoebe Cole of Crosswicks, who predeceased him at their Waker

George Ashby grave marker(Joseph G. Bilby)

Avenue home in Allentown. In January 1944, a reporter interviewed the old veteran, who predicted an allied victory in World War II and stated that if he could, he would "enlist all over again." When George Ashby died in Allentown on April 26, 1946, he was the last surviving New Jersey Civil War veteran. He had 9 children, 16 grandchildren, 14 great-grandchildren and 7 great-great- grandchildren at the time of his death at the age of 102. Ashby received a military funeral complete with color guard and firing squad provided by Hamilton Township American Legion Post #31 and was buried in the Allentown A. M. E. church cemetery. (Bilby, *Forgotten Warriors*)

Joseph G. Bilby

Cornelius S. Barkalow was born near Ardena, Howell Township, New Jersey, in 1842. On July 31, 1862, he enlisted in Company A of the 14th New Jersey Infantry. The six-foot-one-and-a half-inch tall farm boy no doubt presented a commanding appearance, and he was appointed first sergeant. In September of 1862, Sergeant Barkalow, along with other men from the 14th, was detailed to guard a group of Confederate prisoners of war in transit to the Union prison at Fort Delaware. Barkalow, noted for his empathy, shared some of his own food with the hungry, ragged captives and subsequently secured them additional rations, medicine and clean clothing.

During the 14th New Jersey's heroic stand at Monocacy, Maryland, on July 9, 1864, Barkalow was wounded and captured. Fortunately for him, he was recognized by an officer who had been a prisoner in his charge two years earlier. The sergeant's kindness was amply repaid as the Confederate secured him prompt medical attention.

According to a story circulated after the war, Barkalow, shot though the body and bleeding internally, was saved by a Confederate surgeon who passed a strip of silk handkerchief through his wound "so as to cause the blood to run out." His military records state, however, that he was injured by "non penetrating G.[un] S.[hot] wd., thorax, left side," casting some doubt on the story. Barkalow, along with other federal wounded, was left on the battlefield after the Confederates moved on. Furloughed from the hospital on September 6, 1864, he was promoted to first lieutenant and returned to the regiment in November. Barkalow was promoted again, to captain, in December. He received a brevet promotion to major for gallantry in the assault on Petersburg, Virginia, in April of 1865 and was mustered out of service in June.

Barkalow returned to civilian life and married Lydia Cooper at her father's farm in Freehold on December 20, 1865. Shortly afterward, he stepped on a rusty nail in his yard. Cornelius Barkalow died of tetanus on February 12, 1866, and was buried in Bethseda Churchyard in Adelphia. (Martin, *The Monocacy Regiment*)

Joseph G. Bilby

Cornelius S. Barkalow grave marker
(Greg Speciale)

Arabella Wharton Griffith Barlow was born in Somerville, New Jersey, on February 29, 1824, and was privately educated in Burlington County. An "item" in New York society in the years before the Civil War, she married Francis Channing Barlow, an attorney ten years her junior, on April 20, 1861, the day after he joined the 12th New York Infantry as a private for three-months service. Arabella's friend, Maria Lydig Daly, characterized her as an "intriguing, clever" woman, but later opined in the pages of her diary that the bride and groom looked like "a young soldier and his mother." In the summer of 1862, Arabella joined the U. S. Sanitary Commission as a nurse. Although separated by their wartime duties, the couple saw each other whenever practical. On two of those occasions Arabella is credited with saving her husband's life.

Arabella Wharton Griffith Barlow

Barlow went on to become colonel of the 61st New York Infantry and, in September 1862, Arabella Barlow arrived at the Antietam battlefield, where her husband, now commanding a brigade, had been severely wounded by artillery fire. Diarist George Templeton Strong, a founder of the Sanitary Commission, noted that "She is nursing the Colonel, her husband (badly wounded), and never appeared so well. Talked like a sensible, practical, earnest, warm-hearted woman, without a phrase of hyperflutination." Arabella continued to nurse Francis throughout his seven-month recuperation.

Arabella also arrived on the field during the battle of Gettysburg, where she again attended her badly injured husband, now a brigadier general, whose division had been overrun on July 1 at a position known to this day as "Barlow's Knoll." The story of her discovery of her husband's condition and subsequent reunion with him evolved into a romantic tale spun in the 1890s by Confederate General John Gordon, but with dubious provenance; it persists in some quarters to this day. Legend aside, however, Arabella did indeed cross Confederate lines during the battle to tend her husband's wounds and once again keep him alive. She brought him home to Somerville, where she cared for him until he recovered six months later.

In early July 1864, Arabella Barlow contracted typhus while caring for hospitalized soldiers at City Point, Virginia. She died in Washington, DC, on July 27, 1864, and is buried in Old Somerville Cemetery. (Brockett & Vaughn, *Women's Work*; Welch, *The Boy General*)

Robert Silverman
Diana Newman

Arabella Wharton Griffith Barlow
grave marker
(Diana Newman)

Nathan Barnert was born in Posen, Prussia (today's Poznan, Poland) on September 20, 1838, and immigrated to New York City with his parents in 1849. In the early 1850s, Barnert left for the California goldfields and then Hawaii, where he became a prospector and then a peddler. Unsuccessful in both ventures, he returned to New York City in 1856 and entered the clothing business.

In 1858, Barnert moved to Paterson, New Jersey, where he opened a retail clothing and tailoring business and began to accumulate real estate. There was a business downturn in Paterson, as elsewhere across industrial New Jersey, in the immediate aftermath of the outbreak of the Civil War in 1861. Trade with the South was cut off, resulting in business failures and significant unemployment, exacerbating the already severe economic dislocation following the "panic" of 1857. Barnert, an unusually perceptive businessman, as well as a budding philanthropist, was quick to realize that the war would provide new markets and jobs, and successfully bid on large Union-army uniform contracts, which put Paterson people back to work while greatly increasing his own wealth.

Nathan Barnert
(Library of Congress)

Barnert, one of a generation of progressive immigrant German-Jewish businessmen, retired in 1878 and became involved in local politics as a reform Democrat. Elected first as an alderman, he became Paterson's first Jewish mayor in 1883, winning the office for a second time in 1887 after being defeated in 1885. During his tenure in office, he donated his entire salary to various charities in the city.

In addition to his political activities, Barnert and his wife Miriam became generous sponsors of numerous Paterson causes, both Jewish and non-denominational. These included the Miriam Barnert Free School, the Barnert Memorial Temple, a home for the aged and orphans, and Barnert Memorial Hospital. In the case of the hospital, Nathan Barnert donated the land and paid the full cost of constructing the facility, which closed in 2008 after 99 years of service to the community. He died on December 23, 1927, at the age of 89, one of the most popular figures in the history of Paterson. A unique individual, it could genuinely be said of him that he used the money he earned through the tragedy of the Civil War to do good for society. His *New York Times* obituary estimated that Barnert had donated over $1 million to Paterson charities, a huge amount of money for the era. (*NY Times* Obituary; Schwartz, *American Jewish Odyssey*)

John Zinn

Clara Barton was born Clarissa Harlowe Barton in Oxford, Massachusetts, on December 25, 1821, the youngest of five children. The idealistic Barton became a teacher and her 1852 visit to an old friend, Mary Norton, then living in Hightstown, New Jersey, led to a teaching job in Bordentown, where she founded one of the first free public schools in the state. As school enrollment expanded to over 600 students, the local school board replaced Barton with a man who was paid more than she was and demoted her to "female assistant." Unhappy with this state of affairs, she relocated to Washington, DC, in 1854 and took a job with the U.S. Patent Office, where harassment from male fellow employees, no doubt coupled with her Bordentown experience, led her to become an early exponent of feminism.

Clara Barton
(Library of Congress)

(National Park Service)

Following the outbreak of the Civil War, Barton collected food and medical supplies for and nursed sick and wounded men, even visiting the battlefields of Fredericksburg and Antietam. The soldiers she personally delivered clothing, cakes and jellies to included Hart Bodine, a formerly rowdy Bordentown student then serving in Company A of the 6th New Jersey Infantry. Bodine was so touched by Barton's generosity that after the war he named his first born daughter Clara Barton Bodine. Throughout the war, Barton corresponded with friends in Hightstown, who forwarded packages through her to their sons and husbands at the front and collected money to support her charitable activities for soldiers.

At war's end, Barton, distressed by the lack of information on soldiers who had simply disappeared in the chaos of conflict, founded the "Office of Correspondence with the Friends of the Missing Men of the United States Army," the first American organization dedicated to discovering the fate of those missing in action. She sought information from veterans on their memories of forgotten fates and burials and, aided by a former Andersonville prisoner, identified most of the dead at Andersonville Prison, where she raised the flag over the cemetery in August 1865.

Andersonville monument to Clara Barton (State of Georgia)

Clara Barton's wartime activities led this former New Jersey school teacher to found the American Red Cross. She lived a long and useful life and died in 1912. Barton is buried in her native Oxford, Massachusetts. Her original Bordentown schoolhouse has been renovated and is open for visitation. (http://www.waymarking.com/waymarks/WM8EE; Rogers, et al., *Clara Barton and Hightstown*; Faust, *Republic of Suffering*)

Thomas R. Burke Jr.

George Dashiell Bayard was born in Seneca Falls, New York, on December 18, 1835, to a prominent family originally from Princeton, New Jersey. The Bayards moved frequently before settling in Woodbury, New Jersey, from where George was appointed to West Point. Upon graduation from the military academy, he was sent west to fight the Plains Indians, reportedly provoking a Kiowa uprising in 1859.

Bayard was serving as a cavalry instructor at West Point when the Civil War broke out. He initially attempted to gain a commission in a New Jersey cavalry regiment but was unable to do so. His family's political connections paid off, however, and he was appointed colonel of the 1st Pennsylvania Cavalry on September 14,

George Dashiell Bayard (Joel Craig)

1861. Bayard was promoted to brigadier general in April, and his brigade, which included the 1st New Jersey Cavalry, faced Stonewall Jackson's forces at Harrisonburg and Port Republic during the Shenandoah Valley Campaign. Given command of the Army of Virginia's Third Army Corps' cavalry brigade in June, Bayard distinguished himself with his dash and bravery, particularly during the initial stages of the battle of Cedar Mountain on August 9, 1862.

In November 1862, Bayard was assigned to command the cavalry brigade attached to the Army of the Potomac's Left Grand Division. He led the brigade to Fredericksburg, Virginia, where, during the ensuing December 13 battle, he was struck in the thigh by a stray Confederate shell fragment (some sources say it was a cannon ball) while standing outside General Franklin's headquarters. Bayard was severely wounded and died the next day, the only casualty his 3,500-man brigade suffered in the entire battle. To complete his bitterly ironic saga, General Bayard was buried with military honors at the town cemetery in Princeton on December 18, initially planned as his wedding day. He was only twenty-seven years old, reportedly the youngest brigadier general in the army at that time. (Bayard, *The Life of George Dashiell Bayard*; Warner, *Generals in Blue*)

Dr. David G. Martin

Myron Holley Beaumont was born the son of a doctor in Lyons, New York, in 1837. In 1856 he enlisted in the Regiment of Mounted Rifles only to be discharged as a minor ten months later. Residing in Rahway in 1861, Beaumont was commissioned a first lieutenant in the 3rd New Jersey Militia and was subsequently appointed as a major in Halsted's Horse. Accounted as one of that lackluster regiment's few efficient officers, Major Beaumont retained his position in the command shakeup that followed when the unit became the 1st New Jersey Cavalry.

Myron Holley Beaumont (USAMHI/MOLLUS)

There always seemed a whiff of scandal about the darkly handsome Beaumont. His wife was reportedly a granddaughter of Peggy O'Neale Eaton, whose controversial coupling broke up President Andrew Jackson's cabinet. Following the Confederate capture of regimental commander Colonel **Percy Wyndham** and the illness of Lieutenant Colonel **Joseph Kargé**, Beaumont commanded the 1st for several months in 1862, performing creditably. His attempt to undermine Kargé, however, whom he falsely accused of cowardice at Cedar Mountain, led to questions about his own character. With Kargé wounded and on convalescent leave and the exchanged Wyndham also absent wounded, Beaumont commanded the regiment again at Gettysburg, where fellow officers questioned his courage in action. Despite all the misgivings, Beaumont was promoted to lieutenant colonel and was wounded at Hatcher's Run in February 1865. Following the death of regimental commander Colonel Hugh Janeway in the Appomattox Campaign, he was commissioned colonel of the 1st in May 1865 and mustered out of service that July.

Beaumont did not adjust well to civilian life. Taking his oldest son with him, he deserted his wife and ran off in the early 1870s with his brother-in-law's wife, a Mrs. Randolf, to Oregon, where he became editor of the Coos Bay *News*. When Mrs. Randolf died, he quickly married a young lady whose parents had the marriage annulled. Undismayed, Beaumont moved south to San Francisco, where he opened an agency to assist veterans in applying for pensions. Unfortunately, he entered into collusion with a pension clerk to defraud the veterans and had to flee when the scheme was exposed. Beaumont ended up in Ukiah, California, where he and a new wife, Lenora Ortenaga, opened a brothel. When federal investigators closed in, Beaumont died, an apparent suicide, of "a dose of morphine sufficient to straighten out a rhinoceros" on February 16, 1878. (Bilby, "Myron Beaumont")

Joseph G. Bilby

Alfred Bellard (Greg Speciale)

Alfred Bellard was born in Hull, England, on March 7, 1843, and immigrated to the United States with his family in the early 1850s. When the Civil War began, he was a carpenter's apprentice in Hudson City (now part of Jersey City), New Jersey, and in August 1861 enlisted in the 5th New Jersey Infantry's Company C. While serving in the 5th, Bellard, like many soldiers, wrote numerous letters home and kept diaries of his daily activities. He fought in the Peninsula Campaign and at Second Bull Run and was severely wounded in the right leg at Chancellorsville in May 1863. After convalescing, yet still unable to return to active duty, Bellard served the remainder of his enlistment in the Veteran Reserve Corps, an organization created to make use of soldiers unable to do active duty in the field, mostly as a military policeman in Washington DC, but also on the skirmish line when General Jubal Early's Confederates threatened the capital in the summer of 1864.

Private Bellard was mustered out of the army on August 19, 1864, and returned to Hudson City, where he married Annie E. Taylor, took up his father's trade of engraver, and served in 1867-1868 as a captain in the 4th Regiment, New Jersey Rifle Corps, a state militia unit. After Bellard's daughter Daisy was born in 1878, his wife's health failed and she died within two years. Bellard's business soon failed as well. In 1881, in declining health himself, he filed for a pension based on his Chancellorsville wound. Bellard died on September 20, 1891, and is buried in Newark's Fairmount Cemetery.

Alfred Bellard's was an unremarkable nineteenth-century life in many ways, but he was rescued from historical anonymity through the survival of an unpublished war memoir, based on his wartime letters and diaries, which he wrote and illustrated in the 1880s. Purchased in an antique shop in 1962, it was edited by noted Civil War scholar David Herbert Donald and published in 1975 as *Gone for a Soldier: The Civil War Memoirs of Private Alfred Bellard*. Unaffected and genuine, Bellard's memoir has become part of the classic literature of the war and the canon of New Jersey Civil War studies, assuring that he will never be forgotten. (Bellard, *Gone for a Soldier*)

Joseph G. Bilby
Thomas R. Burke Jr.

Jacob Bender, an immigrant shoemaker born in Württemberg, Germany, in 1822, was living in Newark at the outbreak of the Civil War. Bender enlisted in the 8th New Jersey Infantry on January 25, 1862, and served with the regiment through the Peninsula and Second Bull Run campaigns. A hernia he suffered before entering the

Drawing names for the draft, 1864. (*Harper's Weekly*)

service led to Bender's disability discharge on January 10, 1863. Since he had not served for two years, he was subject to the military draft that took place in New Jersey beginning in 1864. Despite his disabled veteran status, Bender was drafted on May 26, 1864, and assigned to Company D of the 15th New Jersey Infantry. He joined the 15th in September and was present at the battles of Winchester, Fisher's Hill and Cedar Creek, as well as the siege of Petersburg, before receiving a second disability discharge on May 16, 1865.

Back in New Jersey, Bender returned to his job in the shoemaking industry, and in August 1866 married twenty-two year old Margaret Conklin in Bloomfield. The Benders were living in Newark in 1870 but later moved to Bloomfield, where Bender lived the rest of his life and the couple had two children. He filed several pension applications, based on his hernia and service-connected rheumatism, although his real problems seem to have been psychological. After Bender's death on April 8, 1889, a neighbor who had known him since 1866 stated that "his mind was then unbalanced, and he was often called 'crazy Jake.' It was commonly supposed that he became so from stresses peculiar to war, or from injury received therein…I met him frequently on the road going to work on and after the above mentioned date and from his irrational and vehement manner of talking became immediately aware of his aberration."

Jacob Bender was buried in Fairmount Cemetery in Newark. (Bilby, *Three Rousing Cheers*).

Joseph G. Bilby

Chester Dawson Berry was born in South Creek (Bradford County), Pennsylvania, on August 1, 1844, the middle child of Harvey and Harriet Berry. His family had been in America since the seventeenth century, and several Berry men fought in the Revolutionary War. By 1861, Berry's family was living on a farm near Battle Creek, Michigan, and in 1862 he enlisted in the 20th Michigan Infantry. Berry was captured at Cold Harbor on June 2, 1864, and was taken to Andersonville Prison. After being released in March 1865, he and many of his fellow Michigan, Indiana, Kentucky, and Ohio comrades were transported to Vicksburg, where they boarded the steamer *Sultana* for the journey home. On April 27, in the middle of the night, seven miles above Memphis, the ship's

Chester Dawson Berry (Pamela Newhouse)

boilers exploded in a spectacular blast, and it burned to the waterline. There were 2,400 former POWs on board. Including the crew and some civilian passengers, over 1,800 people died, making the *Sultana* sinking the worst maritime disaster in United States history.

Sultana (Pamela Newhouse)

Chester Berry survived the *Sultana*, but the experience deeply affected him for the rest of his life and he wrote and talked about it extensively. He began collecting remembrances of the disaster from fellow soldier passengers and in 1892 published *Loss of the Sultana and Reminiscences of Survivors*. He became a minister of the gospel, married, and had a son and a daughter. When Berry's wife died in 1913 he remarried. When his second wife died, he went to live with his son in Theodore, Alabama, where he ministered at a local church and, at some point, inexplicably took off for New Jersey, where he settled for the rest of his life. In 1925, Berry was living at the Arthur Pitney Comfort Home in East Orange. He died on November 22, 1926, and was buried in Glendale Cemetery in Bloomfield. Although the plot is listed in cemetery records, there is no grave marker of any kind. It seems that Chester Berry died as he had lived: humbly and without fanfare. (Newhouse, "Sweet Hour of Prayer")

Pamela Newhouse

William Birney, brother of Union general David Bell Birney, was born on May 28, 1819, in Madison County, Alabama. He was the son of James G. Birney, a Southern slaveholder who became a prominent abolitionist and died in **Rebecca Buffum Spring**'s Raritan Bay Union community at Perth Amboy in 1857. An attorney, Birney practiced law in Cincinnati and then lived in England and France, where he wrote articles and participated in the French Revolution of 1848. He returned to America in 1853 and founded the Philadelphia *Daily Register* newspaper.

At the outbreak of the Civil War, Birney enlisted in the 1st New Jersey Infantry as captain of Company C. He was promoted to major of the 4th New Jersey Infantry in September and became the 4th's colonel in January 1863. In May 1863, he was appointed colonel of the 2nd United States Colored Infantry, and then promoted to brigadier general of volunteers. Birney left direct command of the 2nd to raise seven more regiments of African-American soldiers in Maryland, significantly expediting the cause of emancipation in that state. He later commanded a division of black soldiers in the Tenth Corps and another in the all African-American Twenty-fifth Corps during the last days of the war. He was promoted to brevet major general on March 13, 1865, and mustered out of service later that year. Birney was the highest ranking of the thirty-seven white New Jersey soldiers who served as officers in the United States Colored Troops.

William Birney (USAMHI/MOLLUS)

Following the war, General Birney lived in Florida and then Washington, where he practiced law, served as U.S. Attorney for the District of Columbia and wrote scholarly articles on a number of subjects, as well as a biography of his notable father. New Jersey black veterans were so impressed with Birney and his record of advocacy on their behalf that they named their Red Bank GAR post after him. General Birney died at his home in Forest Glen, Maryland, on August 14, 1907, and was buried in Oak Hill Cemetery in Washington. (Warner, *Generals in Blue*)

Joseph G. Bilby

Charles Stewart Boggs was a native and lifelong resident of New Jersey. He was born in New Brunswick on January 28, 1811, into a family that included his mother's brother, Captain James Lawrence of War of 1812 "Don't Give up the Ship" fame, perhaps predisposing him to a career at sea. Boggs was appointed a midshipman in the United States navy in 1826 and commissioned a "passed midshipman" (ensign) six years later. A lieutenant during the Mexican War, he distinguished himself leading small-boat raiding expeditions. Following the war, he left active duty and commanded several civilian ships.

Charles Stewart Boggs (John W. Kuhl)

The Civil War brought Boggs back to active service and in December of 1861 he was assigned to command the 1,300-ton steamer *Varuna,* the fastest ship in Admiral David Farragut's fleet. The *Varuna* led the way up the Mississippi River in the 1862 federal operation against New Orleans, and Boggs' vessel was attacked by two large rebel ramming ships. Locked in mortal combat and giving as good as he got, he kept his guns firing until the *Varuna* sank but had the satisfaction of seeing both enemy craft destroyed as well. Boggs' sacrifice of the *Varuna* cleared the way for the rest of the Union fleet to sail up the Mississippi unimpeded and capture the Crescent City. He returned to Washington hailed as "the hero of New Orleans" and received presentation swords from both his home city and the state of New Jersey. For the next year Boggs commanded a ship on blockade duty in the Atlantic. In 1864 and 1865, he was back in New Jersey superintending the construction of steam picket boats of his own design, one of which, under Lieutenant William B. Cushing, attacked and destroyed the Confederate ram *Albemarle.*

Boggs fires his "last broadside" as the Varuna sinks.
(*Frank Leslie's Illustrated Newspaper*)

Boggs was promoted to commodore in 1866, retired from the navy in January 1872 as a rear admiral and died at home in New Brunswick from the effects of a stroke on April 22, 1888. In an uncharacteristic statement in that euphemistic Victorian era, his *Army/Navy Journal* obituary described him as "...of a bulldog class of seamen and it is said of him that in moments of excitement he used language bordering on the profane." (Cogar, *Dictionary of Admirals*)

John W. Kuhl

14

George A. Bowen was born in Salem, New Jersey, on September 15, 1843, and enlisted in the 12th New Jersey Infantry's Company I as a sergeant in August 1862. The 12th, serving in the Army of the Potomac's Second Corps, had its baptism of fire at Chancellorsville in May 1863, and Bowen frankly confided his pre-combat anxieties in his diary. They proved out as the regiment was outflanked and overrun, suffering numerous casualties. In late June, the 12th moved north, pursuing the Confederate army into Pennsylvania. The regiment marched across the Bull Run battlefield, where Bowen was appalled by weathering skulls and bones rain-washed out of hasty graves.

George A. Bowen (John W. Kuhl)

12th NJ monument on Cemetery Ridge, Gettysburg (Henry F. Ballone)

The 12th arrived at Gettysburg's Cemetery Ridge on July 2. In a series of vicious fights that afternoon and the following morning, the regiment captured then retreated from a barn between the lines. Late on July 3, the 12th played a crucial role in repulsing Pickett's Charge. The Jerseymen suffered heavily at Gettysburg and Bowen, in the thick of the fighting on both days, barely avoided death or injury. On one occasion, a fencepost he was carrying was stuck by a bullet and on another an artillery round hit a tree he was leaning against, instantly killing the man next to him. Attempting to aid the wounded of both armies at the end of the battle's third day, Sergeant Bowen despaired at the piles of mangled men strewn along the Emmitsburg Road, in some places two to five deep.

Bowen was promoted to first sergeant after Gettysburg and first lieutenant in April 1864. That spring, the 12th was thrown into the maelstrom of the Wilderness, Spotsylvania, and Cold Harbor, and the siege of Petersburg. Remarkably, George Bowen survived it all without a scratch, although his diary graphically records the stress of the campaign, including listening to the cries of the wounded left between the lines for days at Cold Harbor. He was promoted to captain in November and in April 1865 the 12th joined the pursuit of General Lee's army to Appomattox. Bowen was only a few months past twenty-one when he was discharged that June. A solid New Jersey citizen-soldier who did his duty without fuss or fanfare, he married and became a jeweler. George Bowen died on March 26, 1917, and is buried at the Old Broad Street Presbyterian Church Cemetery in Bridgeton, New Jersey. (Bowen Diary; Longacre, *To Gettysburg and Beyond*)

Lesley-Ann Thomson

John Boylan maker's mark inside a fatigue jacket. (Don Stoops, Sharpsburg Arsenal)

John Boylan was born in Ireland in 1822. He immigrated to Newark, New Jersey, sometime prior to 1843, as he was living in the city as of that date. In 1847, Boylan opened a retail clothing store at 214 Broad Street and moved his business to 296 Broad Street in 1851, when his brother James joined the firm, which became known as J & J Boylan. In 1853, Boylan expanded his operations, opening a second retail store in Paterson. Unfortunately, both businesses failed the following year. The two brothers held a variety of other jobs at different Broad Street locations throughout the remainder of the decade, John as a salesman and agent for other clothiers and James as a fabric cutter.

Once the Civil War began, the Boylan brothers reunited as business partners, combining their areas of expertise to become one of the largest Union army uniform contractors of the war. The Boylans' Newark operation produced almost one million garments and other cloth items for the government, a total that included 584,000 "fatigue" or "sack" coats manufactured between September of 1862 and October of 1864. The brothers manufactured and sold everything from fancy Zouave jackets to overcoats, as well as haversacks and rubberized "gum" blankets. With the end of the war, however, their prosperity bubble burst. James left the partnership and John downsized the remaining operation considerably.

In 1869, John Boylan relocated his shop to 139 Grand Street in New York City, while still maintaining his residence in Newark at 701 High Street. Boylan & Company's sales decreased sharply over the next decade, creating a fiscal crisis for the firm. Although James McKenny, another New York military goods dealer, co-signed a loan to help keep the company afloat, Boylan defaulted on payments, forcing McKenny into bankruptcy. In 1878, as Boylan's suppliers began to seek judgments against him, his son Jonathan and son-in-law Eugene Ward joined the company and reorganized it as Boylan Manufacturing Company. The new entity survived until 1903, when it was bought out by Walter Rhodes. John Boylan's date of death is unknown. (Bazelon & McGuinn, *Directory of American Military Goods and Makers*)

Thomas R. Burke Jr.

Walter Morrel Bramhall was born in New York City on August 3, 1839. His family moved to Jersey City in the early 1840's and became well established there, as the city's present Bramhall Avenue attests. As an adult, Bramhall moved to Rahway, New Jersey. With the outbreak of war in 1861, he recruited Jerseymen in Rahway to serve in an artillery battery but unfortunately discovered that New Jersey was not enlisting artillery units at that time. Bramhall took his men to New York City, where they joined Company K of the 9th New York State Militia on June 15, 1861. The Rahway men were among a large number of New Jerseyans who fought in units credited to other states during the war. In 1876, New Jersey Adjutant General **William S. Stryker** claimed a total of 8,957 such out-of-state enlistments during the course of the conflict.

Walter Morrel Bramhall
(Cowan's Auctions, Inc.)

Company K was intended to be an artillery battery serving as an integral part of the otherwise all-infantry 9th. Mustered in as a second lieutenant, Bramhall commanded a two-gun section of the battery, which was initially stationed at Harpers Ferry, Virginia, and was involved in the Union disaster at Ball's Bluff in October 1861. The battery was detached from service with the 9th in August, and in December was formally redesignated as the 6th New York Independent Battery. In January 1862, following the discharge of battery commander Captain Thomas Bunting, Bramhall was promoted to captain and assumed command of the unit. Under Bramhall, the 6th saw action at Williamsburg, Yorktown, Dispatch Station, Malvern Hill and Fair Oaks during General McClellan's Peninsula Campaign in the spring of 1862. After commanding the battery for close to a year, Captain Bramhall resigned on February 3, 1863, citing as his reason the army's failure to meet his supply needs. He died on December 28, 1913, and is buried at Rahway Cemetery. (Foster, *New Jersey and the Rebellion*)

Thomas R. Burke Jr.

Reginald Heber Breintnall was born in Philadelphia on August 18, 1843, moved to Newark with his family four years later and was educated at Newark Academy. In 1860, he became a charter member of the Eureka Base Ball Club of Newark, the premier New Jersey baseball team of the 1860s. Breintnall went on to play for the Eureka in each of the club's nine seasons, including at least one game in the two periods of his Civil War military service. From June 23 through August 1, 1863, he served in Company D of the New Jersey Volunteer Militia unit raised for the "Pennsylvania Emergency" occasioned by the Gettysburg Campaign. In September 1864, he reenlisted as a private in Company K of the 39th New Jersey Infantry and was quickly promoted to Quartermaster Sergeant. Breintnall served with the 39th through to the end of the war.

Reginald Heber Breintnall
(New Jersey State Archives)

After the war, Breintnall enlisted in the 1st Veteran Regiment of the New Jersey Militia, which became a unit of the New Jersey National Guard when the Guard was created out of the Militia and the New Jersey Rifle Corps in 1869. In 1898, along with the rest of the 1st New Jersey Regiment, he volunteered for service in the Spanish-American War, serving as lieutenant colonel of that regiment. In 1902, Breintnall's military career reached its summit when he was promoted to brigadier general and named Adjutant General of New Jersey. General Breintnall was legislatively forced to retire in 1905, but subsequent litigation returned him to his position and he served until 1909.

In addition to his athletic ability on the baseball diamond, Breintnall was an avid hunter, trap shooter and an expert rifleman who won forty-two marksmanship medals at the National Guard's Sea Girt rifle range. He was also active in veterans' affairs both in New Jersey and nationally. In his home state he served on the Board of Managers of the New Jersey Home for Disabled Soldiers in Kearny and was active in Phil Kearny Post #1 of the GAR. The old soldier's long life ended on July 3, 1925, and he is buried in Newark's Mount Pleasant Cemetery. Interestingly, his obituaries provided full reports on his military career, but failed to mention his pioneering role in New Jersey baseball history. (Luzky, *Adjutants General of NJ*; *NY Times* Obituary; Zinn, "History of the Eureka Base Ball Club")

John Zinn

Frederick Amzi Brill was born on November 9, 1836, in New York City. Brill was a house carpenter by profession and lived in Woodbridge for twenty years prior to the outbreak of the war. In August of 1861 he enlisted in the 5th New Jersey Infantry and was made a corporal in Company H. He was twice wounded, in the foot and jaw, at the battle of Williamsburg, Virginia, in May of 1862. The latter wound occurred during the regiment's retreat, when he was hit in the back while hunched over. The bullet passed through his back and ended up in his jaw. Army surgeons could not find the bullet, but while he was at home recovering from his wounds, Brill was attended by Doctor Abernathy of Rahway, a local physician who located the ball and extracted it.

When Corporal Brill returned to his unit at Harrison's Landing, Virginia, in July of 1862, he was promoted to second lieutenant of Company I. On August 29, 1862, at the battle of Second Bull Run, Virginia, he was wounded once more and while being carried from the field was wounded yet again. His second wound proved mortal this time and Brill was left to die on the field near a position that was later overrun by the enemy. Whether he was ever buried or where has never been established. His family erected a cenotaph memorial to him in Rahway Cemetery. (Eckhardt & MacAvoy, *Our Brothers Gone Before*; *Trenton Times*).

Robert F. MacAvoy

Frederick Amzi Brill's government marker is inscribed with "5 NY," the incorrect regiment.
(Diane C. MacAvoy)

Henry Willis Brown was born Henry Barnes in Boston in 1816. In 1839, Barnes abandoned his last name, his wife Susan and his trade as a shoemaker, ran off to Philadelphia and joined the United States army as Henry Brown. He quickly acquired another wife, Rebecca Pierson, a widow with three children. Rebecca traveled with her husband to his various duty stations until his discharge in 1844. The couple then returned to Philadelphia, where they opened a soap and candle factory. Brown took off alone for California in 1852, but returned broke, angry, and given to fits of verbal and physical abuse, according to Rebecca.

Henry Willis Brown (John W. Kuhl)

In the opening months of the Civil War, Brown was appointed a captain and commander of Company A of the 3rd New Jersey Infantry, enlisted in Woodbury. He was soon promoted to lieutenant colonel of the 3rd, and then, in May 1862, colonel, leading the regiment in the Peninsula Campaign, and at Second Bull Run, Antietam and Fredericksburg. While commanding the First New Jersey Brigade due to the absence of General A. T. A. Torbert at Salem Church in May 1863, Brown was wounded and sent home on convalescent leave, returning to duty later in the year. When Torbert transferred to the cavalry in 1864, Brown resumed command of the brigade but was not promoted to brigadier general. He was relieved of brigade command in May 8, 1864, for not moving the unit into action fast enough at the battle of Spotsylvania, was wounded once again on May 12 and mustered out of service in June 1864.

Back home, Brown repeatedly quarreled with Rebecca, and one night in 1869 started breaking up their furniture in a fit of rage, ran out the door and never returned. Returning to Boston, he looked up his first wife, now calling herself "the widow Barnes," who dismissed him. In 1873, while working at the Boston Navy Yard, Brown passed himself off as a forty-five-year-old bachelor and married twenty-five-year-old Marian Smith, giving him three wives at once. He filed a pension claim in 1876, which was contested by Rebecca, but Brown claimed they were never legally married. On his death in October 1892, Rebecca and Marian both claimed survivor benefits, causing confusion among pension bureau officials well into the twentieth century. (Bilby, "An Officer and a Gentleman...Sort Of")

Joseph G. Bilby

Josiah Johnson Brown, a descendent of John Brown, one of Newark's original English settlers, was born in that city on August 29, 1839. He graduated from Rutgers in 1860 and was enrolled as a theological student there when he enlisted in the 2nd New Jersey Infantry as a private on October 1, 1861. He fought in all the regiment's campaigns until he was discharged to reenlist for another three-year hitch as a "veteran volunteer" on February 29, 1864. He believed the coming spring campaign would end the war and took advantage of the thirty-day home leave and generous bounties being offered by county, state and federal governments for those soldiers who reenlisted or "veteranized." When the men of the 2nd who did not reenlist were discharged in May 1864, Brown and other reenlisted men were temporarily transferred to the 15th New Jersey Infantry. Brown fought with that regiment until he was captured in a rear guard action south of Winchester, Virginia, on August 17, 1864.

Josiah Johnson Brown
(Special Collections and University
Archives, Rutgers University Libraries)

Private Brown was confined as a POW at Lynchburg and Danville, Virginia. Although his imprisonment was not pleasant, Danville was far superior to the dreaded Andersonville. Food was short and lice were plentiful, but the prisoners were sheltered in a heated building. Brown was exchanged on February 22, 1865, and, after a convalescent leave, rejoined the reorganized 2nd New Jersey and was mustered out of service with that regiment on July 11, 1865.

Following the war, Brown resumed his theological studies at Union Theological Seminary in New York. On June 17, 1868, he married Mary E. Wilcox. The couple had four children. After ordination as a Presbyterian minister in October 1868, Brown moved west, where he founded the first Presbyterian Church in Independence, Kansas. He subsequently returned to Newark, studied law and was admitted to the bar in 1888.

Josiah Brown lived to become one of the last survivors of his regiment, the sole survivor of the Rutgers class of 1860, and the oldest Rutgers alumnus living before he died in his 80 Hillside Avenue home in Newark on January 20, 1936. He was buried in Evergreen Cemetery in Hillside. A typescript copy of his army reminiscences, written in 1885, is in the collections of the New Jersey Historical Society and provides an important primary source on his regiment. (Bilby, *Three Rousing Cheers*; Brown Memoir; *NY Times* Obituary)

Joseph G. Bilby

Enos Goble Budd was born in Budd Lake, New Jersey, on August 5, 1835. Budd considered careers in medicine and law, but a desire to see "the Indians and...life on the western plains" led him to visit a brother in Minnesota in 1856. He then served as a wagon train leader and army wagon master in the Utah "Mormon War" of 1857-1858, learned the Shoshone language and moved to California, where he worked as a miner and rancher. While leading a party returning east in 1861, Budd fought Apaches in Arizona and was detained as a suspected Yankee spy in the newborn Confederacy. Released, he returned to his native state and in August 1862 joined Company F of the 15th New Jersey Infantry at Roxbury. His army experience, demonstrated leadership and reputation as a crack shot made him an invaluable asset to the regiment in its early days, and he was quickly promoted to first sergeant

Enos Goble Budd in
March 1864.
(John W. Kuhl)

Budd participated in all the 15th's battles through Spotsylvania, where, during a reconnaissance mission on May 9, 1864, he fell wounded in five places. Evacuated to Ward General Hospital in Newark, Sergeant Budd continued to be carried on the regimental rolls as "absent wounded." Promoted first lieutenant of Company C in absentia, he never rejoined the regiment and was not officially "mustered" in that rank. Budd was discharged for disability on June 7, 1865, and shortly afterward commissioned a second lieutenant in the Veteran Reserve Corps. After serving as an assistant provost marshal in Virginia, he was discharged on October 31, 1866.

His military career over, Enos Budd returned to Budd Lake with a disability pension. He became involved in state and local politics and held a number of offices, was active in the GAR, ran an ice business, invented a "revolving water wheel" and authored a book titled *Nature's Working.* In 1881, he married Mary Dyer of Utica, New York. The couple settled in Budd Lake and had four children. Budd, whose wife had predeceased him, died on February 2, 1907. Described as "very liberal" in his religious views and "a charitable man of broad humanitarian principles," he was buried at the Baptist Church Cemetery in Mount Olive. His death certificate listed his profession as "veteran soldier." (Bilby, *Three Rousing Cheers*)

Joseph G. Bilby

Enos Goble Budd after the war.
(John W. Kuhl)

George Childs Burling was born on February 17, 1834, in Burlington County, and was educated at a private school in Norristown, Pennsylvania. Burling was a successful coal merchant and local militia officer in April 1861, when his company was mustered into service for ninety-days service in the 4th New Jersey Militia. In September, Burling returned to active duty as captain of Company F in the newly formed 6th New Jersey Infantry. Promoted to major of the 6th in March 1862 and lieutenant colonel in May, he served as second-in-command of the regiment in the Peninsula Campaign and at Second Bull Run, where he was wounded. When the 6th's Colonel **Gershom Mott** was promoted to brigadier general and command of the Second New Jersey Brigade in September, Burling succeeded him as colonel of the 6th and led it in the battles of Fredericksburg and Chancellorsville, where he was wounded again, as was General Mott.

George Childs Burling
(USAMHI/MOLLUS)

Colonel Burling commanded the brigade at Gettysburg, where, on July 2, 1863, his regiments were placed in reserve near Trostle's Woods and, as the Third Army Corps cracked under Confederate attack, were dispatched to plug gaps in the line from the Emmitsburg Road through the Peach Orchard, over the Wheatfield and down to Devil's Den. The brigade suffered 513 casualties as the Third Corps was rolled back to Cemetery Ridge. On July 3, Burling's brigade was deployed in support of the federal artillery during Pickett's Charge.

On General Mott's return to duty in late August, Burling returned to command of the 6th New Jersey, but in March 1864 he resigned his commission, feeling slighted by a perceived lack of recognition for his Gettysburg efforts. Perhaps to his surprise, one year later, however, he received a brevet promotion to brigadier general "for gallant and meritorious services in the Battle of Gettysburg, Pa." After the war, Burling worked for the Pennsylvania Railroad until his death on Christmas Eve, 1885 of lung cancer. He was buried in the Trinity Section of Camden's Harleigh Cemetery. His presentation sword is part of the Gettysburg National Park Visitor's Center collection. (Bilby & Goble, *Remember You Are Jerseymen*)

Thomas R. Burke Jr.

Garrett Smock Byrne was born in 1836 in Middletown Point (today's Matawan), New Jersey, and was a Newark attorney at the outbreak of the Civil War. When New Jersey raised new regiments to meet a federal troop call in the summer of 1862, recruiting areas were assigned geographically. The 13th New Jersey Infantry, composed of recruits from the state's northeast, was organized at Newark's Camp Frelinghuysen.

Garrett Smock Byrne (Thomas R. Burke, Jr.)

After the war, the 13th's Colonel **Ezra A. Carman** sarcastically recalled that he knew many people "anxious to do duty" as officers, but considerably fewer willing to be privates. He wrote that "for the position of Quartermaster alone I had 87 applicants." Quartermaster was a popular job, since a regimental supply officer was in considerably less danger in battle than a line officer, and some applicants were manifestly unqualified. In 1862, James A. Yard, supervisor of Camp Vredenburgh in Freehold, received a letter from a Long Branch man offering as his qualifications for a quartermaster slot: "I can't run very fast, but I can eat my allowance."

Despite the ineptness of some candidates, the quartermaster served a vital function in any unit, reflecting the truth of Napoleon's maxim that "an army travels on its stomach." Requisitioning, organizing and delivering adequate rations to the troops, who were often on the move, was a complicated task, with some danger from Confederate guerilla raiders as well. Something in Garrett S. Byrne's resumé apparently appealed to Carman. Byrne was commissioned a first lieutenant and appointed quartermaster on August 25, 1862.

Byrne proved an efficient and faithful quartermaster, and in March 1865 received a brevet promotion to captain for his stalwart service. He mustered out with the 13th in Washington on June 8, 1865. On June 10, the regiment's survivors arrived home in Newark, where they were greeted by cheering citizens and a brass band. Byrne appears to have made a seamless transition to civilian life and soon reopened his Broad Street legal practice. By the 1890s, however, with his health failing, he moved into the New Jersey Home for Disabled Soldiers and died there on October 15, 1895, of uremia. He is interred on the top of the hill in the Byrne family plot at Matawan's Rose Hill Cemetery. (Bilby & Goble, *Remember You Are Jerseymen*)

Thomas R. Burke Jr.

Charles Lochiel Cameron was born April 13, 1815, at Tynemouth, near Newcastle, Northumberland, England. He joined the British army's 26th Regiment of Foot and served in Ireland, Gibraltar, Montreal, Quebec, and many other posts, retiring after twenty years of service. He then immigrated with his family to Wisconsin, where he taught foreign languages, and then to Illinois. The outbreak of the Civil War found Cameron in Louisiana, where he joined the Confederate army's 7th Louisiana Infantry as a captain. At the battle of Port Republic, Virginia, in 1862 he was wounded in the throat. He was wounded again, this time in the chest and head, by artillery fire in September 1862 at the battle of Sharpsburg

Charles Lochiel Cameron (Dale C. Caragata)

or Antietam. While leading his company up Cemetery Hill at Gettysburg, Cameron was wounded yet a third time, hit by a bullet that smashed his left collarbone and passed downward through his body, lacerating his left lung.

Postwar view of Port Republic, where Cameron received his first wound. (USAMHI)

Shortly after the war, in 1865, Cameron moved north again and settled in Newark, New Jersey, where he resumed teaching foreign languages and lived for the next thirteen years until the bullet from his Gettysburg wound, which was never extracted, formed an abscess on his lung and caused his death on June 30, 1878. Cameron is buried in Fairmount Cemetery in Newark. (Correspondence with Cameron family; Eckhardt & MacAvoy, *Our Brothers Gone Before*)

Robert F. MacAvoy

Ezra Ayers Carman (John Kuhl)

Ezra Ayers Carman was born at Oak Tree, near Metuchen, New Jersey, on February 27, 1834. In 1849, Carman became a clerk in the Rahway Post Office and in 1850 a clerk for the Farmers Bank of Rahway. He entered the Western Military Institute at Drennon Springs, Kentucky, as a cadet on September 13, 1853, graduated in 1855, then taught there as an assistant professor of mathematics, earning his A.M. degree from the University of Nashville in 1858. By 1861, Carman had returned to New Jersey and was employed as a bookkeeper at T. P. Howell's Newark leather factory.

After witnessing the first battle of Bull Run as a civilian, Carman enlisted and was commissioned lieutenant colonel of the 7th New Jersey Infantry in September 1861. He served with the regiment until the battle of Williamsburg, Virginia, on May 5, 1862, where he was severely wounded in the right arm. While home recovering from his wound that August, Carman was commissioned colonel of the 13th New Jersey Infantry, then forming at Newark's Camp Frelinghuysen. Colonel Carman led his barely trained new unit onto the Antietam battlefield on September 17, where the regiment held its own, while suffering over 100 casualties. The 13th subsequently saw action at Chancellorsville and Gettysburg before being transferred to Tennessee. Carman commanded a brigade in the Atlanta Campaign and during Sherman's March to the Sea, and also served as military governor of Tullahoma, Tennessee, for a period. He was promoted to brevet brigadier general on March 13, 1865, and mustered out of service on June 8.

After the war, General Carman wrote a highly regarded book that is still considered a standard reference on the history of the Antietam Campaign. From 1865 to 1870, he was in the lumber business at Newark and Jersey City and was comptroller of Jersey City from 1871 to 1875. In 1877, he moved to Washington to become chief clerk of the U. S. Department of Agriculture, serving through 1885. Carman was a member of the Antietam Battlefield Board from October 1894 to July 1898 and Chairman of the Chickamauga - Chattanooga National Park Commission from July 8, 1905, until his death from pneumonia in Washington, DC, on Christmas Day, 1909. He is interred at Arlington National Cemetery. (Bilby & Goble, *Remember You Are Jerseymen*)

Thomas R. Burke Jr.

Roderick A. Clark was born in Point Pleasant, New Jersey, on January 25, 1844. A boat builder and "waterman," Clark joined Company F of the 14th New Jersey Infantry as a private in August 1862. He was promoted to corporal in January 1864 and served with the 14th until the July 9, 1864, battle of Monocacy, where he was severely wounded. Clark was hit by two bullets, one of which shattered his left leg below the knee as the other drilled through his right lung. While his regiment retreated and Corporal Clark lay wounded, a Confederate infantryman used his body for cover and a rifle rest. When the Rebel fired, Clark's face was singed by powder burns and he narrowly missed being hit again when a Yankee bullet killed the Rebel.

Clark was left on the field by his Confederate captors and eventually brought to a Union field hospital. His leg wound necessitated amputation and he was hospitalized for the rest of the war. Discharged from De Camp General Hospital in New York in September 1865, he returned to Point Pleasant with an $8 a month disability pension and resumed his boat building trade. In 1879, Clark purchased a piece of property on the Manasquan River. As the railroad pushed south along the Jersey coast, the spot came to be known as Clark's Landing and was a popular tourist attraction, with rentals of Clark-built boats for fishing and crabbing. The highlight of each summer season was the 4th of July celebration, when the peg-legged old soldier put on a memorable fireworks display, although perhaps not as memorable for him as one he had witnessed in an earlier July.

Active in veterans' affairs, Clark was treasurer of the committee that erected a monument to the 14th at Monocacy Battlefield and dedicated it on July 11, 1907. He outlived two wives and one of his two children, dying on November 9, 1929. He was buried at Whitelawn Cemetery in Point Pleasant. (Martin, *The Monocacy Regiment*)

14th New Jersey Veteran reunion badge (Jeff Thompson)

Joseph G. Bilby

14th New Jersey Monocacy Monument, erected in 1907. (Jeff Thompson)

Edmund Janes Cleveland was born in Elizabeth on November 25, 1842, and educated in Pennsylvania and at the Collegiate School in Elizabeth. He enlisted in the 2nd New Jersey Infantry in May 1861 but was discharged for disability a month later. Recovering, he reenlisted in the 9th New Jersey Infantry in August 1862. The 9th, nicknamed the "Jersey Muskrats," after successfully charging through a swamp during the battle of Roanoke Island, was unique among New Jersey units, serving most of its time in the Carolinas.

Although only a private, Cleveland made a significant contribution to New Jersey's Civil War history through his diary, currently in the collections of the New Jersey Historical Society. The diary, much of it published in a series of articles in the Society's *Proceedings* in the 1950s, is a significant primary source. Cleveland was

Edmund Janes Cleveland (John W. Kuhl)

also a prolific wartime letter writer, once writing the *New Jersey Journal* to complain that the "shoulder strap gentry" occupied too much room on a troop transport carrying the 9th, which earned him a reprimand from his company commander.

Despite this transgression, Cleveland was a good soldier, and in 1864 he was detailed for clerical duty with the provost marshall of Beaufort, serving there through April 1865. Returning to New Jersey on reenlistment furlough that winter, he was promised a commission if he produced a certain number of recruits, but he failed to do so. At the end of the war, Cleveland's comrades were so stunned by the news of Lincoln's assassination they thought it a Rebel ruse. He noted that "the boys" believed "[General Joseph] Wheeler's Cavalry cut the telegraph and transmitted this message to mislead us." Private Cleveland was mustered out on June 14, 1865.

A civilian again, Cleveland graduated from the Mercantile College of Newark and then married Elizabeth Bragaw in 1866. The couple had five children, two of whom survived to adulthood. He became secretary of the Elizabeth and Newark Horse Railroad Company, then manager of the Dime Savings Institution and finally director of the National Fire and Marine Insurance Company. Cleveland had an intense interest in coin and medal collecting and became a renowned numismatist, as well as a respected genealogist. He was active in the GAR and a life member of the New Jersey Historical Society. Cleveland moved to Hartford, Connecticut, in 1885, where he died in 1902 and is buried there in Spring Grove Cemetery. (Bilby & Goble, *Remember You Are Jerseymen*; Cleveland, "Early Campaigns")

Sylvia Mogerman

Albert Spelling Cloke was born in 1835 in Kent, England, and immigrated to the United States with his family in 1848, settling in Monmouth County, where in 1853 his father opened a store in Morganville. Cloke attended school in Middletown Point, studied law in Freehold and opened a legal practice. In September 1862 he was commissioned captain of the 29th New Jersey Infantry's Company H, and during his service with the regiment wrote frequently to his brother William, editor of the Freehold *Herald & Inquirer*. The 29th spent its nine-month service performing routine duties in the rear area of the Army of the Potomac. The regiment came under fire once, while crossing the Rappahannock River in May 1863. Two shells hit the 29th, wounding four men, one of them mortally. Towards the end of Cloke's service he was arrested, court-martialed for fraternizing with the enemy and dismissed from the service.

Despite his prior dismissal, in January 1864 Cloke was commissioned as captain of the 3rd New Jersey Cavalry's Company B. The 3rd was also known as the "1st US Hussars" and the "Butterflies," due to its colorful and unique European-style uniforms. Although many troopers deserted on the way to the front, the regiment eventually gained a solid reputation after fighting well at Winchester and Cedar Creek, Virginia.

Cloke was court-martialed again in March 1864 after leaving his company to reconnoiter the premises of a Charles Town, West Virginia, saloon. Charged with disobedience of orders, being drunk on duty and conduct unbecoming an officer, he was dismissed from the service again, but managed to have this sentence revoked a year later. He was honorably discharged from the 3rd New Jersey Cavalry on August 1, 1865.

After the war, Cloke moved to Jersey City, married, had two children and resumed his legal career. He became active in Republican Party politics, was one of the founding members of the Lincoln Association of Jersey City, and gained a reputation as an "interesting and magnetic" speaker on the GAR lecture circuit, specializing in talks on "Little Phil" Sheridan.

Cloke died suddenly on March 4, 1890, in a seedy Jersey City hotel and was buried at the Jersey City and Harsimus Cemetery on Newark Avenue. (Bilby & Goble, *Remember You Are Jerseymen*; *NY Times* Obituary; military service and pension records)

Albert Spelling Cloke grave marker lists the 23rd NJ. His regiment was actually the 29th. (James M. Madden)

Thomas R. Burke Jr.
James M. Madden

Horace Newton Congar was born in Newark on July 31, 1817. He worked as a schoolteacher while studying law and was admitted to the bar in 1847. A dedicated abolitionist, Congar maintained a law office only briefly, however, giving up his practice to devote more time to the anti-slavery movement. One of the founders of the Free Soil Party in New Jersey, Congar was a delegate to the party's 1848 convention that nominated Martin Van Buren for president. He subsequently joined the new Republican Party and was a delegate to the 1860 Republican convention, supporting front-runner William Seward for the nomination.

Horace Newton Congar
(New Jersey Historical Society)

Although Abraham Lincoln was chosen over Seward and other candidates, Congar enthusiastically supported the Republican ticket in New Jersey. He had a readily available means with which to express his support as he had been the editor of the Newark *Daily Mercury* since 1850. Described as the leading Radical Republican newspaper in New Jersey before the Civil War, the journal was not very popular in Newark or around the state. With a circulation of only about 1,500, the *Daily Mercury* was only kept afloat through loans from Republican and abolitionist supporters.

Abraham Lincoln appointed Congar as U.S. Consul to Hong Kong and he spent most of the war years in that position. On his return to the United States, he moved to Washington when Lincoln appointed him Commissioner of Immigration. With the election of fellow Republican **Marcus Ward** as Governor, Congar returned to New Jersey, where he served as Secretary of State from 1866 to 1870. He subsequently entered the insurance business with the Mutual Benefit Company. His long tenure with Mutual Benefit was interrupted by one other period of public service, when he served as U.S. Consul to Prague in 1873. Horace Congar died in Newark on January 25, 1893. (Congar Papers; Siegel, *For the Glory of the Union*)

John Zinn

Stephen Crane (Library of Congress)

Stephen Crane was born in Newark on November 1, 1871, more than six years after the end of the Civil War. As author of the most famous novel about the conflict, however, he is perhaps the most well known New Jerseyan associated with the war. Crane and his family moved to Port Jervis, New York, in 1878, but on his father's death two years later the Cranes returned to New Jersey, settling in Asbury Park, where Stephen's brother Townley ran the *New York Tribune* bureau. In 1891 Stephen inherited Townley's "On the Jersey Coast" column. Crane as columnist proved an entertaining writer but public relations disaster. His criticism of eccentric Asbury Park founder James A. Bradley and the city's tourist business led to the *Tribune* firing both Cranes. Stephen moved to New York to work as a free-lance journalist and author, and published his first novel, *Maggie: A Girl of the Streets*, in 1893.

Crane's Civil War saga, *The Red Badge of Courage*, was published in 1895. The twenty-three-year-old author created what he termed "a psychological portrayal of fear" in Henry Fleming, a young Union soldier whose dreams of glory evaporate as he deserts his regiment's line of battle to escape the horror of combat. Fleming redeems himself after being clubbed by a fleeing fellow Yankee and sheepishly returning to the line, where his bloodstained, bandaged injury is taken for a bullet wound by his fellow soldiers and becomes a "badge of courage" prompting his subsequent heroic redemption.

Crane wrote his masterpiece without experiencing combat himself. Although a military school stint provided him with an introduction to army life, he also discussed the war with participants, most of them probably New Jerseyans. Many veteran reunions were held in Asbury Park, which also had its own GAR post. One of Crane's journalism assignments was covering New Jersey National Guard target shooting and skirmish drills at Sea Girt. There he would have seen soldiers shoot and maneuver and had the opportunity to rub shoulders with New Jersey veterans, from common soldiers to Medal of Honor recipients like General **William Sewell** and Captain **J. Madison Drake.**

Crane went on to become a war correspondent and author of other highly regarded novels before dying of tuberculosis at a German spa on June 5, 1900. He is buried in Hillside's Evergreen Cemetery. (Bilby & Ziegler, *Asbury Park*; Lurie & Mappen, *Encyclopedia of New Jersey*)

William B. Styple

John Joseph Craven (USAMHI/MOLLUS)

John Joseph Craven was born in New York City on September 8, 1822. His family moved to Newark when he was nine. While working in the 1840s as a master carpenter for Samuel F.B. Morse, then running a telegraph line from Newark, Craven developed a type of *gutta percha* insulation that Morse used. Craven was not paid for this innovation. Leaving Morse in disgust, he headed to California as a "'49er," but returned to New Jersey to his wife and two children and decided to become a doctor. After apprenticing with a Newark physician, Craven opened his own practice in 1858.

When the Civil War began, Craven became surgeon of the 1st New Jersey Militia and subsequently applied to the United States Army Volunteer Medical Corps. Although his appointment was opposed by the Essex District Medical Society because he was not a medical school graduate, Craven passed an army examination and was appointed as brigade surgeon to General Horatio Wright's command on Tybee Island, Georgia. Capable and affable, he rose to become chief medical officer of the Department of the South, with headquarters on Hilton Head Island, and in 1864 he was appointed chief medical officer of the Department of Virginia and North Carolina. When captured Confederate president Jefferson Davis was brought to Fortress Monroe as a prisoner, Craven was assigned as his personal physician. He was promoted to brevet lieutenant colonel in March 1865 and mustered out in January 1866.

Craven is most famous for his authorship of the 1866 book *The Prison Life of Jefferson Davis* (believed largely ghost written by his friend, Charles G. Halpine), which treated the former Rebel leader sympathetically and characterized his treatment as inhumane. The book became a best seller and was largely instrumental in gaining Davis' release as well as earning Craven some financial security. A civilian once more, Doctor Craven moved to Jersey City, where he practiced medicine and supervised the cleanup of a slaughter house that posed a public health menace. Returning to invention, he received three patents, including one for refrigeration units using recycled iced water that were used to store American beef on ships bound for Europe. Craven retired to Patchogue, Long Island, and founded a free library there. He died in Patchogue on February 9, 1893.
(http://www.civilwarsurgeonsmemorial.org/; Mappen, *Jerseyana*)

Valerie M. Josephson

Charles Curie was born in France on October 20, 1842, and came to Paterson with his parents in 1844. In 1856, he moved to Cleveland to apprentice in a relative's store, but returned to New Jersey in 1859 and began work for an importer, handling the firm's relations with the New York customs office.

In April 1861, Curie enlisted in the 9th New York State Militia, also known as Hawkins' Zouaves, one of a large number of Jerseymen enlisting in out-of-state units. At Roanoke Island in February 1862, he was first to reach the enemy breastworks, waving the regimental colors. The 9th also saw action at the battles of Second Bull Run, South Mountain and Antietam, where Curie was wounded. Subsequently commissioned a second lieutenant in the 178th New York Infantry, he participated in the Meridian Expedition in Mississippi and the Red River Campaign in Louisiana, where he served as brigade ordnance officer. Promoted to captain in September, he became seriously ill in November and was sent to the Jefferson Barracks Hospital in St. Louis. Curie was medically discharged on December 16, 1864, although he was not released from the hospital until March of 1865. Still ill, he returned to Paterson, where his mother nursed him back to health.

Charles Curie
(John Kuhl)

Charles Curie returned to work in January 1866 and partnered with Julius Binge to open his own customs-house brokerage business two years later. He later moved from Paterson to Brooklyn, studied law and was admitted to the New York bar in 1882. Well positioned to advise clients on tariff law, he became a partner in Curie, Smith & Mackie, which became the largest tariff specialty practice in New York City. Curie was also very active in veterans' affairs, with membership in the Union League and other organizations. He served as Chancellor of the Military Order of the Loyal Legion in 1899 and was New Jersey GAR Department Commissioner in 1905-6.

On May 9, 1910, Curie visited the offices of Hoboken-born Doctor Adele Cuinet, a pioneering Brooklyn woman dentist whose parents were friends of his, and was stricken in the dental chair by an apparent heart attack. When the efforts of Doctor Cuinet and her associate failed to revive him, a nearby physician was called and declared him dead. He was buried in Paterson, where a bust statue of him still stands. (http://all-biographies.com/soldiers/charles_curie.htm; *NY Times* Obituary)

Thomas R. Burke Jr.

Charles Curie
Bust in Paterson.
(Henry F. Ballone)

William Lewis Dayton was born on February 17, 1807, in Basking Ridge, New Jersey. He attended the Trenton Academy and graduated from Princeton University in 1825, studied law, and was admitted to the New Jersey bar in 1830. He practiced law in Freehold and in 1833 married Margaret Elmendorf Van Der Veer. The couple had seven children.

Dayton embarked early on a political career and was elected to the New Jersey legislature in 1837. He subsequently served as an associate judge of the New Jersey Court of Errors and Appeals (Supreme Court). After resigning from the court in 1841, Dayton re-entered private law practice briefly and the following year was appointed a U.S. senator

William Lewis Dayton (Library Of Congress)

by Governor William Pennington to fill out the term of deceased senator Samuel L. Southard. A member of the Whig Party, he was elected senator for a full term by the New Jersey legislature in 1845, but failed reelection six years later. In 1856, Dayton, by then a Republican, edged out Abraham Lincoln to be the party's first vice presidential candidate, running on a ticket with John C. Fremont.

After the electoral defeat of Fremont, Dayton became New Jersey attorney general but remained involved in Republican politics on a national level and campaigned enthusiastically for Lincoln in the election of 1860. Following his inauguration, President Lincoln appointed Dayton the United States minister to France, where he is credited with successfully convincing the government of Napoleon III not to recognize the Confederacy's independence or give Confederate vessels the rights to use French ports. Dayton died of a stroke in office in France on December 1, 1864. His body was returned to New Jersey and was buried in Trenton's Riverview Cemetery. (Lurie & Mappen, *Encyclopedia of New Jersey*)

Joseph G. Bilby

Charles Dunham Deshler was born in Easton, Pennsylvania, on March 1, 1819, but moved to New Brunswick, New Jersey, as a child. At the age of 13, he graduated from the Rutgers preparatory school and was apprenticed into the pharmacy business, ultimately becoming a drug store owner. Originally a Whig, Deshler became very active in the virulently anti-Catholic and anti-immigrant "Know Nothing" party before becoming a Democrat. Switching careers, he became the editor of the *American Standard,* and then left that paper for an editorial position with the Newark *Daily Advertiser.*

Although not a strong supporter of the war, Deshler provided an invaluable service to many New Jersey soldiers and their families in the summer of 1864. During the Atlanta Campaign, a large number of men from New Jersey regiments were treated for wounds and disease in western hospitals, and the distance from the state made it extremely difficult for officials and families to communicate with the men, much less attend to their care. Deshler was appointed a state military agent by Governor **Joel Parker** and spent at least two months visiting some 275 hospitalized soldiers in Tennessee and Kentucky. In addition to arranging furloughs, pay, clothing and other necessities, he provided New Jersey newspapers with soldiers' addresses, which were printed so that their families could contact them.

Charles Dunham Deshler
(Courtsey of Special Collections and University Archives, Rutgers University Libraries)

After the war, Deshler returned to New Brunswick, where he was active in civic, business, and educational affairs, becoming known as the founder of that city's public school system. He also performed literary work for Harpers and wrote two books on poetry. Deshler's long life ended in New Brunswick on May 10, 1909, at the age of 90. ("Obituary of Charles Deshler"; Zinn, *The Mutinous Regiment*)

John Zinn

Dorothea Lynde Dix was born on April 4, 1802, in Hampden, Maine (some sources give her birthplace as Worcester, Massachusetts). A lifelong social progressive, Dix opened a school when she was but fourteen-years-old herself. Self-educated through extensive reading, she established several other schools in the following years and authored seven books. Dix's intense work schedule reportedly caused her health to break, however, and she went to England to convalesce.

Dorothea Lynde Dix (David Martin)

Once back in the United States, Dorothea Dix became a pioneering crusader for the rights and treatment of the mentally ill, particularly those in poverty, and especially in Massachusetts and New Jersey. Her 1843 work, a "Memorial to the Legislature of Massachusetts," recommending the establishment of mental hospitals, has been called "the first piece of social research" in America. A similar "Memorial" to the New Jersey legislature resulted in the opening of the "New Jersey Lunatic Asylum" in 1848. Dix was also a strong advocate of prison reform and education for the blind.

During the Civil War, Dix was named superintendent of female nurses for the Union army, a post she organized with her usual efficiency, although her subsequent administrative skills came into question. Dix's judgment was not error free either, as her assumption that New Jerseyan **Cornelia Hancock** would not be a good nurse was proved dramatically incorrect. Despite those shortfalls, she incontestably ranks as one of the greatest social reformers in American history. After the war, Dix lived in Trenton on the grounds of the New Jersey Asylum (now known as the Trenton Psychiatric Hospital) she had helped to establish. During her life, she founded or expanded over thirty mental institutions across the country. Dix died, unmarried, in Trenton on July 17, 1887. She was returned for burial to Cambridge, Massachusetts, at Mount Auburn Cemetery. (Lurie & Mappen, *Encyclopedia of New Jersey*)

Dr. David G. Martin

Decatur Dorsey was born into slavery in Howard County, Maryland, in 1836. Dorsey was a laborer in Baltimore when he was freed to join the 39th United States Colored Infantry in March 1864. The regiment was assigned to guard supply trains against Confederate guerillas from May through June, and, as part of the Ninth Army Corps' all African-American Fourth Division, took part in the siege of Petersburg, Virginia.

The 39th's most desperate fight occurred on July 30, 1864, at the "Battle of the Crater," when a Union effort to capture Petersburg with a huge mine explosion and follow-up infantry attack failed dismally. Instead of using his well-trained black division, which was eager to fight, to

Decatur Dorsey grave marker
(Henry F. Ballone)

spearhead the attack, General Ambrose Burnside ordered his three badly battered white divisions forward first. When they bogged down, the Fourth Division was ordered to save the situation.

The situation was beyond saving, and chaos among the thousands of soldiers milling around the huge crater was compounded by an aggressive Confederate counterattack. Some regiments, including the 39th, pushed through towards their objective, then found themselves cut off and retreated. Dorsey, a "color sergeant" in the 39th, was entrusted with carrying a regimental battle flag, indicating he was held in high esteem by his officers and comrades. The job was fraught with danger, as the flags or "colors" of a regiment were symbolic of its honor and enemy fire concentrated on the color party. Under heavy small arms fire, Dorsey planted his flag on the Confederate defenses and then, when his comrades retreated, waved it vigorously to rally and reorganize them. For his courageous actions, Dorsey was awarded the Medal of Honor in November 1865, when his regiment was on occupation duty in North Carolina.

Dorsey was mustered out as a first sergeant with his unit in North Carolina in December 1865 and subsequently moved north with his wife, Mary Christy Dorsey. In 1870, the Dorseys were living in New York City but then moved to Hoboken, New Jersey, where they were living on Jefferson Street with Mrs. Dorsey's mother, Rachel Christy, and a seven-year-old boarder, Mary Startler, in 1880. Dorsey, who worked as a laborer and sailor, spent the rest of his life in New Jersey, dying in Hoboken on July 11, 1891. He is buried in Flower Hill Cemetery in North Bergen. (http://www.hmdb.org/marker.asp?marker=5756; Bilby, *Forgotten Warriors*)

Joseph G. Bilby

Alexander N. Dougherty was born in Newark, New Jersey, in January 1822 to Alexander and Sarah Congar Dougherty. Dougherty's father was a prosperous leather merchant who secured an excellent education for his son. After attending private schools in Newark, Dougherty received an A.B. degree from Oberlin College in 1841 and later received an A.M. from Princeton University. He attended Albany Medical College for one year and completed his studies at the College of Physicians and Surgeons in New York. After receiving his medical degree in 1845, Dougherty returned to Newark, where he established a practice and lived until the outbreak of the Civil War.

Alexander N. Dougherty
(New Jersey State Archives)

In August 1861, Dougherty was appointed surgeon of the 4th New Jersey Infantry, and the following month he was commissioned into the United States Volunteer Medical Corps and elevated to brigade surgeon of Brigadier General **Philip Kearny**'s First New Jersey Brigade, where he served until 1862. Surgeon Dougherty was appointed to the position of medical director of the Army of the Potomac's Second Army Corps following the battle of Antietam, and later also of the Ninth Army Corps. He was wounded at the May 1864 battle of Spotsylvania. But he returned to duty and in 1865 was appointed chief medical officer and medical director of the First Veteran Corps of the Army of the Shenandoah by General Winfield Scott Hancock, whose wound Dougherty had personally attended during the repulse of Pickett's Charge at Gettysburg. In December 1864, Dougherty was awarded the rank of brevet lieutenant colonel for "meritorious and distinguished services during the campaign before Richmond, Virginia," and in October 1865 was promoted to brevet colonel and mustered out of the service shortly thereafter.

Dougherty returned to his native Newark after he left the service and became an attending surgeon at the newly established St. Barnabas Hospital, a member of several area medical societies and delegate to American Medical Association conventions. He also served as vice-president of the College of Physicians and Surgeons Alumni Association. Doctor Dougherty died on November 28, 1882, of heart disease, leaving a widow, Henrietta, and four living sons. He was buried at Mount Pleasant Cemetery in Newark following a funeral attended by General Hancock and his staff. (*The Biographical Encyclopedia*)

Valerie M. Josephson

James Madison Drake was born in Washington Valley, New Jersey, in 1837. A precocious young man, Drake became a journalist at an early age and was publisher of the Trenton *Evening News* by 1857. In April 1861, he joined Company C of the 3rd New Jersey Militia as a sergeant. Mustered out in July, Drake reenlisted in Company K, 9th New Jersey Infantry, as a sergeant in October 1861, eventually rising to the rank of first lieutenant.

Drake was captured while commanding part of the regiment's skirmish line at the battle of Drewry's Bluff on May 16, 1864. He later made a daring escape while being transferred from one prison to another in South Carolina and, with the aid of slaves, safely made his way over hundreds

James Madison Drake (John W. Kuhl)

of miles to Union lines in Tennessee. Drake was subsequently awarded the Medal of Honor for his heroic actions during the Bermuda Hundred Campaign of 1864. Mustered out of service in 1865, Drake moved to Elizabeth and reentered the newspaper world, subsequently publishing the Elizabeth *Daily Monitor*, *Sunday Leader* and *Daily Leader*. He was a prolific book author as well, with a number of works to his credit, including a history of the 9th New Jersey and *Fast and Loose in Dixie*, an account of his dramatic POW escape.

Drake and his Veteran Zouaves at Sea Girt, 1908. (John W. Kuhl)

Drake was also active in the New Jersey National Guard. He served as colonel of the 3rd Regiment for five years and convinced the state legislature to make him a brevet brigadier general before resigning. In the late 1870s, Drake returned to the Guard as a captain commanding a Gatling gun company. The company, which Captain Drake ran without regard to state regulations, served as a home for his nationally known "Veteran Zouaves" drill team and marching society until it was finally disbanded in 1892 for enlisting overage and overweight recruits and failure to wear regulation uniforms. The Veteran Zouaves continued to tour the country for years afterward, however, and appeared at a GAR encampment at Sea Girt in 1908. Drake, one of nineteenth-century New Jersey's most colorful characters, died at his home in Elizabeth on November 28, 1913, and was buried in Evergreen Cemetery in Hillside. (Bilby, *Sea Girt: A Brief History*; *NY Times* Obituary)

Joseph G. Bilby

Thomas Haines Dudley was born in Evesham Township, New Jersey on October 9, 1819. He was admitted to the New Jersey bar in 1845, practiced law in Camden and, as Camden County Clerk, wrote the city charter of Camden. Originally a Whig, Dudley was one of the founders of the state Republican Party. An abolitionist, he personally raised $1,000 to ransom a Camden County black family kidnapped into slavery, then traveled south himself, posing as a slave trader, to effect their rescue. An early supporter of Abraham Lincoln, Dudley spearheaded Lincoln's nomination at the 1860 convention and was rewarded by the president with the post of U. S. consul at Liverpool, England, in 1861.

Thomas Haines Dudley
(Phil Cohen, DVRBS.com)

Laird Ram (*Harper's Weekly*)

Early on, the South saw Great Britain, its major raw cotton customer before the war, as a source of weapons, equipment and other manufactured goods the Confederacy lacked, and quickly dispatched buyers to Britain to purchase goods and sleek blockade-running vessels to ship them in. Dudley just as quickly initiated efforts to checkmate the Rebels, eventually establishing a network of over 100 undercover agents who provided intelligence on shipments of war material, which he then passed on to the U.S. navy. Dudley's legal action filed in a British court against the sale of the steamship *Alexandra* in 1862 ultimately failed, but made Queen Victoria's government more sensitive to enforcing neutrality laws, which tied up the sale of the far more dangerous ironclad "Laird Rams," being built in Birkenhead. Dudley remained consul in Liverpool through 1872, and played a role in the settling of the *Alabama* claims, in which Britain paid compensation for the destruction caused by that British-built Confederate commerce raider.

Thomas Dudley eventually returned to Camden, where he became president of the local bar association and the New Jersey Agricultural Society, as well as a number of businesses. He also wrote numerous articles on agriculture, trade, tariffs, politics and international relations, and conducted friendly debates with Walt Whitman. Dudley died of a heart attack in Camden on April 15, 1893, and is buried at Colestown Cemetery near Moorestown. (http://www.dvrbs.com/people/DVRBS-Camden-Biographical.htm; Lurie & Mappen, *Encyclopedia of New Jersey*)

Joseph G. Bilby

Samuel Francis DuPont was born on September 27, 1803, in today's Bayonne to a French family unsuccessful in early New Jersey real estate ventures but later the leader of the American gunpowder and chemical industries. DuPont was appointed a navy midshipman at age twelve and reported for his first sea duty in 1817. Rising rapidly through the ranks, he was cited for both shore operations and for capturing an enemy brig during the Mexican War.

Samuel Francis DuPont (Library of Congress)

In 1861, DuPont, a captain with an interest in steam propulsion and extensive experience on various naval boards, was one of the most influential naval officers on active service. He was one of the principal architects of the blockade strategy intended to strangle the South and led successful federal naval operations in the Carolinas in late 1861. When the navy created the rank of admiral in July 1862, DuPont was commissioned a rear admiral, second in seniority among active duty officers, an event that became the high point of his career.

Admiral DuPont's monitors attack Charleston.
(*Frank Leslie's Illustrated Newspaper*)

Encouraged by the early success of ironclad ships, Secretary of the Navy Gideon Welles ordered DuPont to capture Charleston, South Carolina, with a naval expedition. Although the admiral replied that such an operation required army support, Welles ordered him to attack with naval forces alone. On April 7, 1863, DuPont led eight ironclads towards the city. The slow-firing monitors got off only 139 shots in the ensuing forty-minute fight while 100 Confederate guns deluged the federal ships with converging fire from around the harbor, averaging ninety hits on each ironclad and forcing DuPont to retreat. He was ordered to attack again, and when he argued against the wisdom of the orders, was replaced. DuPont's judgment was confirmed when subsequent naval efforts to take Charleston failed dismally. He never again held an important post, however, and died in a Philadelphia hotel room on June 23, 1865, of diphtheria and bronchitis. Samuel F. DuPont was buried near his home outside of Wilmington, Delaware. (Merrill, *Dupont: the Making of an Admiral*)

John W. Kuhl

James Ezekiel Emerson was born in Maine on November 2, 1823, and worked as a farmer, sawmill operator and carpenter in his youth. In 1850, he established a factory for making woodworking machinery in Lewiston, Maine. Emerson was an inventor as well as manufacturer, and developed a machine for boring, turning, and cutting spools and bobbins used in the cotton-weaving process, an operation that had previously required three separate machines. In 1852, Emerson followed the Gold Rush to California, where he acquired a number of sawmills and began to develop a new concept for producing circular saw blades. Leaving California to return east, Emerson settled in Trenton, New Jersey, where he founded the Malleable Iron Works.

At the outbreak of the Civil War, Emerson joined with Joseph S. Silver of Philadelphia's Keystone Edged Tool Works to form the Emerson & Silver Company in Trenton. Emerson & Silver successfully competed for large military contracts for all kinds of swords, as well as bayonets, scabbards, spades, camp hatchets, felling axes and handles, totaling nearly 100,000 units, making the company one of the largest contractors of its type during the war.

The Emerson & Silver mark on a sword blade. (Ron Ruble)

In 1866, Emerson & Silver, one of the most famous and profitable wartime contractors, was dissolved as Emerson returned to more peaceful pursuits. He founded the American Saw Company, with its manufacturing facility in Trenton and an office in New York City. At the 1867 Paris Exposition, American Saw exhibited its new $2,000 eighty-eight-inch circular saw. Emerson filed for a number of patents, including a combination anvil/shears, a punching machine and a swage for spreading saw teeth to a uniform width, shape and cutting edge in a single operation. The innovations he brought to the saw blade industry provided the template for today's woodworking saws. As saw sales grew, Emerson opened a satellite sales office in San Francisco to accommodate demand. The American Saw Company was acquired by the Rubbermaid Corporation in 2003 and is still in business today. James Ezekiel Emerson died in 1900 in Columbus, Ohio, and was buried at Riverview Cemetery in Trenton. (Bishop, *A History of American Manufactures*; Herringshaw, *Herringshaw's National Library*)

Postwar Emerson saw blade advertisement.
(*Scientific American Magazine*)

Thomas R. Burke Jr.

42

John Young Foster was born in Clinton, New Jersey, on June 19, 1831. Foster lived in Hunterdon County until 1846, when he moved to Somerville and entered the newspaper field. He initially took a position with the Newark *Daily Mercury* before moving to New York City to become editor of the New York *Mail*. He was working as an editor with *Harper's Weekly* when Republicans in Newark tried to start a new paper to replace the *Daily Mercury* after it closed in 1863. Anxious about possible competition, Thomas Kinney, the owner of the Newark *Daily Advertiser*, negotiated with this group to see if his paper might meet their needs. While the specific outcome of the negotiations is unclear, John Foster was named editor of the *Daily Advertiser* and held that position until the end of the war.

John Young Foster
(*Philadelphia Inquirer*)

A staunch Unionist, Foster was reportedly a "brilliant extemporaneous speaker" in great demand for political events. His considerable oratorical skills were called into play when news of Lincoln's assassination reached Newark. Foster delivered a eulogy for the martyred president at South Park (soon to be re-named Lincoln Park), which was still vividly recalled at the time of his own death some thirty years later. In June of 1866, Foster became the editor of the Newark *Evening Courier*, a Radical Republican newspaper that lasted into the 1870s. Shortly after the Civil War, there was significant demand for a book that would relate and preserve the memory of the role New Jersey soldiers played in the conflict while also refuting criticism that the state did not do her part in supporting the Union. After a joint session of the state legislature authorized Governor **Marcus Ward** to appoint someone to write such a chronicle, Ward chose Foster. The editor spent a year writing *New Jersey and the Rebellion*, which was published in 1868. Foster's royalties were reportedly used to build his home on Newark's Stratford Place.

Following the demise of the *Evening Courier,* Foster became an editor of *Frank Leslie's Weekly*, where he remained for seventeen years. He also stayed politically active, serving as secretary of the Republican State Committee for about a quarter of a century. Foster died at home on November 13, 1896, from pneumonia reportedly brought on by overwork for the Republican Party in the 1896 national election. (*Newark Daily Advertiser;* Siegel, *For the Glory of the Union*)

John Zinn

Louis Raymond Francine was born on March 26, 1837, in Philadelphia, Pennsylvania, reportedly descended from an old and noble French family. Francine's French-born father was traveling the world in 1826 when he decided to settle in Philadelphia, where he married Catherine Lohra. Shortly after Louis' birth, the Francine family moved to Camden, New Jersey. Young Francine spent much of his youth in France and in 1856 entered the *Ecole Polythechnique* in Paris to study engineering. He returned to America in 1858 and was working as a civil engineer when the Civil War began. In the summer of 1861, he was commissioned a captain after raising a unit in Cape May County that became Company A of the 7th New Jersey Infantry.

Louis Raymond Francine (USAMHI/MOLLUS)

Captain Francine proved to be an excellent officer and hard drillmaster. He was promoted to lieutenant colonel of the 7th on July 8, 1862, and colonel of the regiment on December 9. The 7th New Jersey was part of the famed Second New Jersey Brigade in the Army of the Potomac's Third Corps, and saw its first action at the battle of Williamsburg, Virginia, on May 5, 1862. The regiment was subsequently heavily engaged during the rest of the Peninsula Campaign, and at Second Bull Run, Chantilly and Chancellorsville.

On July 2, 1863, at the battle of Gettysburg, the regiments of the Second New Jersey Brigade were fed into the fight independently to shore up the Third Corps line, which was under heavy enemy pressure. The 7th was deployed east of the Emmitsburg Road near the Peach Orchard as a support for Union artillery, including New Jersey's Battery B. The battery and the regiment were forced to retreat as the Union lines on their flanks crumbled. Colonel Francine kept his regiment under control but was wounded as he withdrew towards Cemetery Ridge. Although Francine's wound seemed serious it did not appear mortal at the time. He died at Saint Joseph's Hospital in Philadelphia on July 16, however, and was buried in Laurel Hill Cemetery in Philadelphia. After the battle, he was posthumously promoted to the rank of brevet brigadier general of volunteers, retroactive to the date of his wound.

In 1888, the 7th New Jersey's surviving veterans erected their Gettysburg monument on the spot where Francine was wounded. It includes the simple inscription, "Colonel Francine fell here." (Francine, *Louis Raymond Francine*)

Dr. David G. Martin

7th NJ monument, Gettysburg (Henry F. Ballone)

Frederick Theodore Frelinghuysen was born in Millstone to an old and distinguished New Jersey family on August 4, 1817. When his father passed away three years later, Frederick was adopted by his uncle Theodore Frelinghuysen, who served as New Jersey's attorney general and a United States senator during his adopted son's adolescence. Theodore Frelinghuysen was also the vice presidential candidate of the Whig Party during Henry Clay's presidential run in 1844. He became president of Rutgers College in 1850 and served in that position until his death in 1862.

Frederick Theodore Frelinghuysen
(Library of Congress)

Frederick Frelinghuysen, better known as "Fred," graduated from Rutgers in 1836 and then studied law at his uncle's Newark office, establishing his own practice in 1839. The well-connected Frelinghuysen represented many important corporate clients, including the Central Railroad of New Jersey and the Morris Canal and Banking Company, and held local political office as well. In 1842, he married Matilda Elizabeth Griswold. The couple had six children.

A Whig, Frelinghuysen left that political party as it disintegrated in the 1850s and joined the newly formed Republican Party. He was a delegate to the 1860 Republican convention and attended the February 1861 "Peace Conference" along with Governor **Charles Olden** and former governor **Rodman Price**. Unlike Price, he had no sympathy with slavery or secession, however, and was a firm Unionist. Newark's Camp Frelinghuysen, from which thousands of Jerseymen went off to war, was named after his family.

During the Civil War, Frelinghuysen served as New Jersey attorney general. He was appointed by Governor **Marcus Ward** to fill a vacant seat when U.S. Senator William Wright died in office in 1866. Senator Frelinghuysen was a Radical Republican and favored African-American suffrage and the impeachment of President Andrew Johnson. Confirmed by the Republican majority legislature in 1867, Frelinghuysen served through 1869, when a Democrat majority in the legislature failed to reelect him. After turning down an offer from President Ulysses S. Grant to serve as ambassador to Great Britain, Frelinghuysen was again elected to the Senate and served from 1871 to 1877. In 1881, he was appointed Secretary of State by President Chester A. Arthur, a position he held until early 1885, when he retired and moved back to his home in Newark. Unfortunately, Frelinghuysen's retirement was brief, as he died on May 20, 1885. He is buried at Mount Pleasant Cemetery in Newark. (Lurie & Mappen, *Encyclopedia of New Jersey*)

Thomas R. Burke Jr.

Samuel Gibbs French was born on a farm near Mullica Hill in Gloucester County on November 22, 1818, and became the highest ranking of three Confederate generals born in New Jersey. Confederate Adjutant General Samuel Cooper was not, as is sometimes cited, born in the Garden State. French placed fourteenth of thirty-nine graduates in his West Point class of 1843, well ahead of Ulysses S. Grant. He fought in the Mexican War, where he was badly wounded and twice cited for gallantry. Following the war, French received presentation swords from both the New Jersey legislature and the citizens of the state. In 1853, he married Matilda Roberts of Natchez, Mississippi. After she and both of her parents died, French, left with an infant daughter, inherited their family plantation.

Samuel Gibbs French
(John W. Kuhl)

When the Civil War broke out, French, firmly entrenched in the Southern aristocracy, unsurprisingly chose to serve the Confederacy. Commissioned a brigadier general in October of 1861, he initially built defensive fortifications and then served as a field commander in Virginia and North Carolina. In late 1862, French was promoted to major general and then transferred to the western theater, where he served as an effective senior commander in the Vicksburg and Atlanta campaigns. He commanded a division at the battle of Franklin in November 1864, but was subsequently forced to resign from the army when afflicted by an eye infection that left him nearly blind.

Unable to resume military duty, French returned to his neglected plantation. Postwar conflicts with Reconstruction authorities led him to move to northern Florida, where he went into the orange grove business. At the outset of the Spanish-American War, French offered his services to President William McKinley but they were declined. At the time of his death in Florala, Alabama, on April 20, 1910, Samuel French was the oldest living Confederate general. He was buried beside his second wife in Saint John's Cemetery in Pensacola, Florida. French's well-written autobiography, published in 1901, provides an insight into the thinking of a New Jerseyan who became a Confederate general and never regretted his decision. (French, *Two Wars: An Autobiography*)

John W. Kuhl

Edward N. Fuller was born in Boston, Massachusetts, in 1824. Fuller later moved to New Hampshire, where he began a long career in the newspaper business, editing a number of periodicals in that state. In 1857, Fuller came to New Jersey to assume editorship of the newly formed Newark *Daily Journal*, a Democratic Party newspaper. Fuller's reputation of having the "strongest Democratic proclivities" made him well suited for the position. Like the Republican *Daily Mercury*, the *Journal* struggled financially, but it had the benefit of financial support from wealthy Newark Democrats.

Edward N. Fuller (Washington State University)

Under Fuller's leadership, the *Daily Journal* was stridently anti-Republican and anti-war, becoming the "object of pure hatred to New Jersey Republicans and almost equally unpopular with many Democrats." Until the *Daily Mercury* went out of business in 1863, there was open warfare between the two newspapers. Fuller finally went too far in July of 1864 when he urged New Jerseyans to resist the Lincoln administration's plans to draft 500,000 new soldiers, writing, among other things, "not a man shall be forced out of the State to engage in the abolition butchery." On July 21, he was arrested for "inciting insurrection" and released on $7,000 bail, and then was presented with a cane-sword by some leading Democrats as a "brave man." Not wishing to make a martyr out of Fuller, the authorities delayed his trial until February 1865, when the Confederacy was collapsing. When the case finally reached trial, Fuller was allowed to plead guilty and pay a $100 fine.

At the war's end, Fuller resigned as editor of the *Daily Journal*, implying that he was forced out by the owners. By 1866, however, he was back in charge and remained the publication's editor until 1871. At that point, Fuller moved to the midwest and ultimately the west, working at newspapers in Illinois, Utah and Washington. He died in 1904. (Gillette, *Jersey Blue*; Siegel, *For the Glory of the Union*)

John Zinn

Michael Gallagher was born in Ireland in 1832. At the outbreak of the Civil War, he was working as a moulder and living in Jersey City with his wife, Mary Doyle

Libby escape tunnel (*Century Magazine*, Courtesy of Gayle Stahlhuth) Gallagher, and son James. In October 1861, Gallagher, like many Jersey City Irishmen, joined the Irish Brigade's 88th New York Infantry. Initially a second lieutenant, he was promoted to first lieutenant and then captain while fighting with the 88th in a series of bloody battles, including Antietam and Fredericksburg. When the depleted New York regiments of the Irish Brigade were consolidated from ten companies each to two in May 1863, Gallagher and other "surplus" officers were discharged.

Gallagher returned to Jersey City and then enlisted in the 2nd New Jersey Cavalry in August 1863. The 2nd had more than its share of ne'er do wells recruited through high-bounty payments, and Colonel **Joseph Kargé** was looking for experienced officers to whip them into shape. Gallagher fit the bill and was given command of Company H. The 2nd was initially deployed in Virginia, where Gallagher ran into a large number of Confederates while on patrol near Harpers Ferry, led a saber charge into the enemy ranks and was captured. He remained confined in Libby Prison, a former Richmond tobacco warehouse used to house captured Union officers, when the rest of the regiment was sent west.

At Libby, Captain Gallagher became a participant in the greatest POW escape in American military history, organized through the inspired leadership and organizational and engineering skills of Colonel Thomas E. Rose and Major Andrew G. Hamilton. On February 9, 1864, after seventeen days of digging led by Rose, 109 officers slipped out of the prison through a tunnel and disappeared into the night. Although only fifty, including Gallagher, made it back to Union lines, the Confederacy's prison bureaucracy was deeply shaken, and remaining prisoners were soon moved further south.

After his dramatic escape, Captain Gallagher returned to active duty with the 2nd. He was shot through the heart and killed while leading a charge at Egypt Station, Mississippi, on December 28, 1864, leaving Mary a widow with three sons. Michael Gallagher was buried at Corinth National Cemetery, Corinth, Mississippi, one of New Jersey's unsung true heroes of the Civil War. (http://richmondthenandnow.com/Tunnel-Escape-from-Libby-Prison.html; Bilby & Goble, *Remember You Are Jerseymen*; Gallagher Pension Records)

Joseph A. Truglio
Joseph G. Bilby

Isaac Gordon was born a slave in Washington, North Carolina, census records giving at least three different birth dates in the 1840s. He lived with his mother in the household of a Methodist minister, and his father was a cobbler owned by a local widow. In the spring of 1862, Washington was occupied by the Union expeditionary forces commanded by General Ambrose Burnside. Edward E. Potter was appointed its military governor, as well as colonel of a newly formed African-American regiment raised from the region's population. As summer approached, young Isaac Gordon was said to have come to these forces with information used to repulse a Confederate attack west of the city at

Raising the Union flag in Washington, North Carolina. (*Harper's Weekly*)

Isaac Gordon's grave marker
(Kate Malcolm, Madison Historical Society)

Tranter's Creek. He later accompanied the Union army as it drove deeper into North Carolina from its coastal strongholds, reportedly acting as guide to a successful cavalry raid in July 1863 led by Potter, then a brigadier general, against Greenville, Tarboro, and Rocky Mount.

After the war, General Potter, a New York native, brought Gordon with him to Madison, New Jersey, where he served as Potter's coachman and servant when Potter wasn't at his second residence in New York. Meanwhile, Gordon made a home in Madison with his locally born wife, Margaret. On June 1, 1889, Potter died in New York City, where he was buried with the fanfare befitting a victorious Union general. Several years later, Gordon married his second wife, Frances, with whom he had a daughter, Edith, while remaining in Madison and working as a day laborer. His wife having left him, Isaac Gordon died alone about April 8, 1917, and was buried in Madison's Hillside Cemetery. Carved into the gravestone is his wartime story, one that he could not have read because as a slave he was not taught to read or write.

(Eckhardt & MacAvoy, *Our Brothers Gone Before*; Gordon gravestone; *NY Times* Obituary; Turvey presentation)

Robert F. MacAvoy
Steven D. Glazer

Gabriel Grant was born in Newark, New Jersey, on September 4, 1826, to Charles and Caroline Grant. His father was a stone and marble cutter and a direct descendant of Robert Treat, one of Newark's founding settlers.

Grant graduated from Williams College in 1846 and the College of Physicians and Surgeons in 1851, then traveled to Panama to study tropical diseases on the Isthmus. Panama, a popular passage to the Pacific for American gold seekers on their way to California, proved a fertile field for such research, with thousands of travelers stricken with yellow fever, malaria, cholera and dysentery. Two years later, Grant returned and assisted New York officials in controlling a cholera epidemic that was ravaging the city, and was then appointed health commissioner of Newark.

Gabriel Grant (John W. Kuhl)

When the Civil War began, Grant was commissioned as the surgeon of the 2nd New Jersey Infantry. After an examination by a U. S. Army Medical Board, however, the highly qualified physician was promoted to brigade surgeon, and soon rose to division surgeon in chief. Grant saw action in the Peninsula Campaign and at Second Bull Run, Antietam and Fredericksburg, frequently exposed to enemy fire in the line of duty. In 1863, he was appointed Medical Director of Hospitals at Evanston, Indiana, and in May assumed command of the steamer *Atlantic*, a fully equipped transport hospital. He was present at the siege of Vicksburg, and General Burnside subsequently placed him in command of Madison US Army Hospital in Indiana. The hospital had 3,000 beds and, at one point, 2,760 patients. Madison's mortality rate of 120 patients (1.66%) during Grant's tenure was an astounding accomplishment for the time. Doctor Grant resigned his commission in January 1865 due to the lingering effects of an earlier wound.

Upon his return to civilian life, Grant married, and he and his wife Caroline had four children. By 1880, he was living and practicing medicine on East 49th Street in Manhattan. In July 1897, Grant retroactively received the Medal of Honor for his conduct at Fair Oaks. His citation noted that he "removed severely wounded officers and soldiers from the field while under a heavy fire from the enemy, exposing himself beyond the call of duty, thus furnishing an example of most distinguished gallantry." Gabriel Grant died on November 8, 1909, and is buried in Sleepy Hollow Cemetery, Westchester County, New York. (*MOH Citation*; *NY Times* Obituary)

Valerie M. Josephson

George Gill Green (NJ State Library)

George Gill Green was born in Clarksboro, New Jersey, on January 16, 1842. In June 1864, he left his studies at the University of Pennsylvania Medical School after two years to enlist as a private, oddly enough considering his family roots, in the 142nd Illinois Infantry, a unit raised for 100-days service. The 142nd was stationed near Memphis, Tennessee, where it performed guard duty on the Memphis and Charleston Railroad, and saw no combat action before being mustered out of service on October 27.

Green never returned to medical school, but established a wholesale drug business in Baltimore after the war. When his warehouse burned down, he moved on to Ohio, where he opened two other wholesale drug companies before returning to Woodbury, New Jersey, in 1872 with his wife, the former Angie Brown. On reestablishing himself in his native state, Green purchased from his father the rights to two patent medicines, "Green's August Flower," purportedly useful in combating "a cold, [or] an affliction of the throat or lungs," and "Dr. Boschee's German syrup," promoted as a palliative for problems of the "stomach and liver". Through clever marketing, using direct mailings of almanacs and flyers, Green turned these products into national brands and they made him one of the richest men in New Jersey.

Green lived the rest of his life in Woodbury, summering at Lake Hopatcong, but he extended his business interests to California, where in the 1870s he purchased a hotel in Pasadena, then considered a health resort, especially for tuberculosis victims, and renamed it the "Hotel Green." Over the years, the hotel grew into a three-unit complex to include the lavish "Castle Green Apartments," where guests could rent luxury suites by the week or the year. The apartments still stand and are on the National Register of Historic Places.

Following the 1906 passage of the Pure Food and Drug Act, which restricted patent medicine vendors from making extravagant curative claims about their products, Green's business began a slow decline. He died in Woodbury on February 26, 1925. (Lurie & Mappen, *Encyclopedia of New Jersey*; Reed, *A State of Health*)

Joseph G. Bilby

One of Green's patent medicine almanacs. (National Institutes of Health)

John Grimes was born in Parsippany, New Jersey, in 1802 into an abolitionist Quaker family. Grimes became a doctor in 1828 and moved to Passaic County to practice, but later moved to Boonton, where he bought a house located at the corner of Main and Liberty Street, in 1832. Although New Jersey, especially in its northern counties, was far from a hotbed of abolitionism, the Grimes family of Morris County and their associates were publicly enthusiastic in the anti-slavery cause. Doctor Grimes, reportedly once arrested for harboring a runaway slave, became a major conductor on the Underground Railroad's New Jersey section and secretary of the New Jersey Anti-Slavery Society. Grimes' obituary noted that escaping slaves passed through "his own home in Boonton…They came to him from Baxter Sayre, Esq. of Madison … he forwarding them in the night to Newfoundland [NJ], the next station."

John Grimes' birthplace in today's Mountain Lakes, NJ. (www.mtnlakes.org)

Grimes was best known for establishing and publishing, between 1844 and 1850, the *New Jersey Freeman*, a newspaper that espoused "religious humanitarianism" causes beyond abolition, including "women's rights, prohibition and socialism," as well as racial equality. He was also an early proponent of animal rights and a founder of the American Vegetarian Society. In the 1840s, Grimes and his fellow abolitionists campaigned to remove the last vestiges of legal slavery from the state and legislatively succeeded in 1846, although New Jersey still counted eighteen aged "apprentices for life," noted as "slaves" in the 1860 census, on the eve of the Civil War.

Grimes became a professed pacifist during the Mexican War but, like **Rebecca Buffum Spring**, made an exception to his pacifism in 1861 to enthusiastically support what he believed to be a just war that would end slavery. His abolitionist nephew, Quincy Grimes, enlisted in the 15th New Jersey Infantry in August 1862 and died of disease in September 1863. Doctor John Grimes died in Boonton in 1875 and was buried in the Boonton Avenue Cemetery. His birthplace, now located in Mountain Lakes, was entered into the National Register of Historic Places on April 4, 1977.
(http://www.mtnlakes.org/History/Hisgrimeshouse.htm; Mitros, *Gone to Wear the Victor's Crown*; Switala, *Underground Railroad*)

Joseph G. Bilby

Sarah Moore Grimké was born on November 26, 1792, and her younger sister, Angelina Grimké Weld, on February 20, 1805, both in South Carolina. The Grimké sisters were raised in a slaveholding family. Both converted to Quakerism, however, and became ardent abolitionists as well as women's rights advocates. The Grimkés were the first women to launch vociferous public speaking campaigns against slavery. The sisters' strong activist stance split the abolition movement into moderate and radical wings in the 1830s. Although Angelina married moderate abolitionist Theodore Weld, her personal radicalism continued unabated. In 1838, the Grimkés' speeches to the Anti-Slavery Convention in Philadelphia spurred rioters to set fire to the hall they spoke at.

Sarah Moore Grimké (Library of Congress)

The Grimké sisters lived in various towns in New Jersey, including Fort Lee, Belleville, Englewood and Perth Amboy, for many years. Their most important contribution to the abolition movement, written during their residence in the state, was the book *American Slavery as It Is*, published in 1839. The work was a ringing indictment of the "peculiar institution," taken entirely from Southern primary sources.

The sisters were deeply involved with **Rebecca Buffum Spring's** revolutionary interracial and coeducational Raritan Bay Union Eagleswood School in the 1850s and actively supported the Union cause following the publication of the Emancipation Proclamation. After the Civil War, the Grimkés moved from New Jersey to Massachusetts and mentored the education of their African-American nephews, sons of their brother and a slave woman who had been enslaved themselves. A great-niece, Angelina Grimké Weld, was a well-known writer in the twentieth-century Harlem Renaissance literature movement. Sarah died on December 23, 1873, and Angelina on October 26, 1879. (Lurie & Mappen, *Encyclopedia of New Jersey*; Switala, *Underground Railroad*)

Joseph G. Bilby

Alanson Austin Haines (John Kuhl)

Alanson Austin Haines was born in Hamburg, New Jersey, on March 18, 1830, to attorney and future New Jersey governor (1848-1851) Daniel Haines and his wife Anna Maria Austin Haines. Haines dropped out of Princeton University in 1851 and worked for several years as a civil engineer before returning to school at Princeton Theological Seminary and graduating in 1858. After serving as a Presbyterian pastor in Maryland and Long Island, he returned to Hamburg in 1862 and was commissioned as a chaplain in the 15th New Jersey Infantry in August. Always concerned about the welfare of the regiment's men, regardless of their religious affiliation, Haines also led stretcher parties to rescue the wounded and tended them right behind the front lines, gaining a reputation as one of the finest New Jersey chaplains. Perhaps his most doleful duty was escorting the remains of his brother **Thomas Haines**, an officer in the 1st New Jersey Cavalry killed in 1862, back to Hamburg from Virginia in 1864.

After mustering out with the 15th in June 1865, Reverend Haines became pastor of the "Old North" or First Presbyterian Church in Hamburg. His pastorate gave him the time to indulge in his scholarly interests, and the veteran chaplain joined the American Palestinian Exploration Society's expeditions to the Middle East in 1873 and 1876. Haines also collected fossils for Princeton University, served as a trustee of Blairstown Academy, wrote articles on local history, and was active in veterans' affairs. In 1883, he authored *History of the Fifteenth Regiment New Jersey Volunteers*, based on his and regimental adjutant **Edmund Halsey**'s wartime letters, notes and diaries.

By the mid-1880s, Haines' health began to decline, and he retired from the ministry in 1890. He died on December 11, 1891. The chaplain's casket, emblazoned with his old First Division, Sixth Army Corps red Greek-cross insignia, was surrounded by an honor guard of twenty New Jersey veterans. Over two hundred former soldiers attended Haines' funeral and the line of carriages on the road to the North Church Cemetery in Hardyston was a mile long. Reverend A. Clark Cline, former chaplain of the 11th New Jersey Infantry, delivered a graveside eulogy, and General William Penrose, the 15th's old commander, then on duty in the regular army, who returned to New Jersey for the funeral, succinctly summed up the chaplain's life: "He was a brave Christian gentleman and what more can we say of anyone." (Bilby, *Three Rousing Cheers*)

Joseph G. Bilby

Thomas Ryerson Haines was born in Hardyston, Sussex County, on March 15, 1838. He was the son of New Jersey Governor Daniel Haines (1848-1851) and a member of Princeton University's class of 1857. With the outbreak of the Civil War, Haines joined the 1st New Jersey Cavalry as a first lieutenant. He was promoted to captain in February 1862. While serving as commander of the regiment's Company M in a charge at Harrisonburg, Virginia, on June 6, 1862, Haines attempted to rally his men, who had been driven back in disarray by a Confederate ambush. The captain drew the attention of a Rebel cavalryman, who shot him in the back with a revolver. It was reported that as Haines lay wounded he was sabered in the head by another Confederate who was in turn cut down by the 1st's Captain Virgil Broderick. Later promoted to lieutenant colonel, Broderick himself was subsequently killed at the battle of Brandy Station in 1863.

**Thomas Ryerson Haines
(New Jersey State Archives)**

Union cavalry advancing in the Shenandoah Valley, 1862. (*Frank Leslie's Illustrated Newspaper*)

Captain Haines was buried near the spot where he fell, but his grave was marked and discovered by his older brother, Chaplain **Alanson Haines** of the 15th New Jersey Infantry, on September 25, 1864, while the 15th was campaigning in the Shenandoah Valley. Chaplain Haines was granted ten days leave to take his brother's remains back to New Jersey for burial in the North Church Cemetery in Hardyston, where Alanson joined him in 1891. (Bilby, *Three Rousing Cheers;* Bilby & Goble, *Remember You Are Jerseymen*)

Robert F. MacAvoy

Edmund Drake Halsey was born on September 11, 1840, in Rockaway, New Jersey, the son of local farmer, gristmill owner and attorney Samuel Halsey and his wife Sarah. He graduated in the Princeton class of 1860, then studied law and enlisted in the 15th New Jersey Infantry as a private and adjutant's clerk in August 1862. He was promoted to sergeant major in January 1863, and then first lieutenant and adjutant in August 1863. Halsey's older brother Joseph, born in 1823, had moved to Virginia before the war and married into the local aristocracy. In May 1861, Joseph joined the Confederate army's 6th Virginia Cavalry as a private. He was promoted to captain in November and appointed an acting commissary of subsistence.

Edmund Drake Halsey
(New Jersey State Archives)

Edmund Halsey served with his regiment through some of the most intense battles of the war, including Spotsylvania, where the 15th was decimated in four days of constant fighting that culminated in a bloody charge on the "Muleshoe" position on May 12, 1864. Halsey resigned his commission due to his father's failing health on December 31, 1864.

Returning to Rockaway, Edmund Halsey completed his legal studies and opened a law office in Morristown in November of 1865. He became a prosperous attorney and bank director, and served as a trustee of the Rockaway Presbyterian Church and the Morris County Children's Home. Politically active as well, Halsey was elected a member of the Rockaway township committee and served one term in the state legislature. Like his friend, Chaplain **Alanson Haines**, Edmund Halsey was a scholar, and in the years after the war became involved in historical and genealogical research and writing.

On May 27, 1869, Halsey married Mary Darcy, a longtime sweetheart he had corresponded with during the war. Halsey was lucky in war, emerging without a scratch from some of the most desperate fights of the conflict, but not, unfortunately, as blessed in his family life. He and Mary had seven children, but only two survived to adulthood and one of those died shortly after graduating from Princeton. Halsey himself succumbed to pleurisy on October 17, 1896, and was buried at First Presbyterian Church Cemetery in Rockaway. His Confederate brother outlived him, dying in 1907. Edmund Halsey's letters and journal, copies of which are in several archival collections, are invaluable resources for the student of the 15th New Jersey and the state's role in the war. (Bilby, *Three Rousing Cheers;* Halsey Journal)

Joseph G. Bilby

Oliver Spencer "Pet" Halsted was born in Elizabeth in 1819, the son of distinguished New Jersey jurist Oliver Spencer Halsted. An engaging youth, he was nicknamed "Pet" by doting aunts. Although a Princeton graduate and attorney like his father, Pet took a distinctly different path in life. After a stint in the California goldfields, he returned to New Jersey and became involved in politics. Halsted never ran successfully for office, but he made it his business to know influential people, and with former Governor William A. Newell providing an entrée, insinuated himself into Mary Lincoln's entourage when the first lady spent the summer of 1861 in Long Branch, and followed her back to Washington.

Oliver Spencer "Pet" Halsted
(The Lincoln Institute)

"Pet" spent the rest of the war in the capital. Although considered a somewhat shady character, Halsted "went everywhere and knew everybody." With access to cabinet officers and the president himself, he became the first big-time lobbyist. When a businessman or inventor wanted to sell something to the government, the New Jersey attorney became the man to see, and Halsted peddled steamships, muskets, artillery and ammunition of varying degrees of effectiveness to the army and navy. In early 1865 he purchased "The Intelligent Whale" a submarine built to clear Charleston Harbor, but rejected by the navy as only of use in "smooth water." Halsey proposed to Lincoln that he and his son be commissioned as naval officers and sail the sub up the James River to Richmond, but the war ended before the project materialized

At war's end, Halsted, arguably the most influential Jerseyman of his day, returned to Newark, where he docked his submarine on the Passaic River, allegedly took it out for an occasional spin and demonstrated it for various potential clients, including former Union general and Irish Fenian rebel activist Thomas Sweeney, before eventually selling it to the navy.

Halsted's "Intelligent Whale" on display at Sea Girt.
(Henry F. Ballone)

Halsted's submarine outlasted him. Although a family man with a large brood of children, he maintained a mistress in an apartment above a Newark saloon, where her jealous former lover shot and killed him in July 1871. Not to be outdone by 21st century tabloids, the *Newark Daily Advertiser* headlined the incident "Shocking Results of Guilty Love, Jealousy, Rum and Passion." Halsted was buried at the Presbyterian Church Cemetery in Elizabeth. In 1872, the navy gave the "Whale" a second trial, which it failed, and then lost interest. It is currently on display at the New Jersey National Guard Militia Museum in Sea Girt. (Bruce, *Lincoln and the Tools of War,* Ragan, "Union Whale.")

Joseph G. Bilby

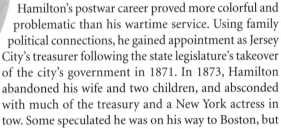

Alexander D. Hamilton was born in March 1844 in Jersey City. He enlisted as a private in the 2nd New Jersey Militia in 1861 and reenlisted as a first sergeant in the 2nd New Jersey Cavalry in 1863. After a shaky start, the 2nd became a reliable regiment under the leadership of Colonel **Joseph Kargé**. Hamilton, promoted to first lieutenant, was mustered out of service at Vicksburg, Mississippi, in November 1865.

Hamilton's postwar career proved more colorful and problematic than his wartime service. Using family political connections, he gained appointment as Jersey City's treasurer following the state legislature's takeover of the city's government in 1871. In 1873, Hamilton abandoned his wife and two children, and absconded with much of the treasury and a New York actress in tow. Some speculated he was on his way to Boston, but Hamilton headed in the other direction. Reports soon placed him in Texas where, following brushes with bandits and corrupt law officers, he crossed into Mexico and fell in with "General" Juan Cortinas, the "prince of all Mexican outlaws."

Alexander D. Hamilton
(New Jersey State Archives)

Jersey City, in the person of police inspector Benjamin F. Murphy, was close behind. Unfortunately, Cortinas was unwilling to turn over Hamilton and Murphy was not in a position to force the issue. Several months later, however, Murphy opened his door to a knock from a ragged, broke and penniless Hamilton. According to the ex-treasurer, Cortinas confiscated his ill-gotten gains and then shipped him out to Brazil.

Following three years in state prison, Hamilton returned to Jersey City and opened "Hamilton's Varieties," a dance hall and saloon eventually shut down by the police. Undeterred, he opened another variety venue on Sixth Avenue in New York City. In 1881, he took to the road again, ending up in Illinois with a new wife and infant son. Employed as a sort of celebrity bartender, he gave a *New York Times* reporter an 1883 interview providing a highly colored account of his road trip to Texas with Jersey City's money.

Deserting his second family, Hamilton went south, settled in Jackson, Mississippi, as a poultry farmer, married another woman and had another child. In 1915, he signed himself into a Civil War veterans' home in Dayton, Ohio, listing his occupation as "traveling salesman," and signed out a year later. Hamilton died on April 12, 1917, but his final resting place is unknown. (Mappen, *Jerseyana; NY Times*; Sackett, *Modern Battles of Trenton*)

James M. Madden

Ellis Hamilton was born on October 15, 1845, in Philadelphia, Pennsylvania, and moved to Camden, New Jersey, at the age of four. Early on, Hamilton developed an interest in military activities and was enrolled as a militiaman while still a teenager. When war came with the spring in 1861, he could not wait to go, but was too young to serve. He was finally mustered in as a second lieutenant of Company E, 15th New Jersey Infantry in 1862, at the age of sixteen. Hamilton, son of a prominent New Jersey newspaper editor, was the youngest New Jerseyan commissioned as an officer and perhaps the youngest officer commissioned in the entire Union army during the Civil War.

Ellis Hamilton (New Jersey State Archives)

Hamilton was promoted to first lieutenant on March 10, 1863, and then captain and commander of the 15th's Company F on November 4, 1863. He was present with the regiment at the battles of Fredericksburg, Salem Church and Gettysburg. When his company was detailed to bury Gettysburg dead in the Wheatfield on July 4, 1863, Hamilton wrote home that he was sickened by the sight of "dead men lying there all bloated up and with faces as black as ink, and pools of blood all around the ground." Worse was yet to come.

View from the Orange Turnpike, with the Wilderness beyond.
(National Archives)

Captain Hamilton was badly wounded through both legs by a single bullet at the battle of the Wilderness as the sun rose on May 6, 1864. He was sent to Seminary Hospital in Georgetown, where he died of his wounds on May 16. He was sorely missed by his regiment. Hamilton's body was returned to Camden for funeral services, after which he was buried in Trenton's Mercer Cemetery. The young officer's letters and other mementos were donated to the New Jersey Collection of the Rutgers University Alexander Library during the Civil War centennial. They are one of the most important surviving sources on the history of the 15th New Jersey. (Bilby, *Three Rousing Cheers*)

Joseph G. Bilby

Cornelia Hancock (New Jersey Historical Society)

Cornelia Hancock, who would become known as the "Florence Nightingale of America," was born on February 6, 1840, to an old New Jersey Quaker family at Hancock's Bridge in Salem County. Hancock was introduced to social work through her brother-in-law, a Philadelphia physician.

As a result of the large numbers of casualties at the battle of Gettysburg in July 1863, the military requested civilian medical assistance. Hancock's brother-in-law answered the call and took her with him, despite the disapproving orders of superintendent of nurses **Dorothea Dix**, who thought Cornelia unsuitable for nursing soldiers because she was too young and attractive. Hancock arrived at Gettysburg two days after the battle and without any official support or supplies, but she helped wherever she could, writing letters for the wounded, praying with them, making them comfortable with blankets and foraging food supplies. Despite her innate dislike of alcohol, she dispensed with scruples and began to serve what would become a trademark "punch" of condensed milk laced with whiskey.

In addition to her material aid, Hancock's cheery mood and optimism did much to raise the morale of her patients, and she quickly became an indispensable army nurse, serving through the winter camp of 1863-1864 and the brutal Overland Campaign of the spring of 1864. Cornelia Hancock was one of the first Union women to enter Richmond after its capture. Although she was particularly highly regarded among the South Jersey men of the 12th New Jersey Infantry, soldiers throughout the Army of the Potomac recognized and cheered her whenever she appeared. The dance tune *The Hancock Gallop* was written in her honor and a medal was cast to commemorate her service.

After the war, Hancock, supported by other Quakers, moved to South Carolina and founded a school for black children that eventually reached an enrollment of several hundred students. After leaving the South for health reasons in 1875, she spent the rest of her life in social work in Philadelphia, and was especially active and successful in Wrightsville, a poverty-stricken neighborhood in the southwest section of the city. Cornelia Hancock died from nephritis on December 31, 1927, at her home in Atlantic City, and was buried at Harmersville. (www.lyoncamp.org; Lurie & Mappen, *Encyclopedia of New Jersey*)

John W. Kuhl

Charles Garrison Harker was born on December 2, 1835, in Swedesboro, New Jersey. Harker worked as a retail clerk for New Jersey First District Congressman Nathan T. Stratton of Mullica Hill, who facilitated a West Point appointment for him. After graduating in the class of 1858, Second Lieutenant Harker was assigned to the 9th US infantry and served at Governors Island, New York, and on the Oregon and Washington frontier.

Following the outbreak of the Civil War, Harker was promoted to first lieutenant and then captain in the 15th US Infantry and assigned to train Ohio volunteers. He was appointed colonel of the 65th Ohio Volunteer Infantry in November 1861. The 65th was assigned to the Army of the Ohio and first saw action at Shiloh. Harker subsequently commanded a brigade at the battles of Perryville and Stone's River. While in command of the Third Brigade in the First Division of the Twenty-first Corps at Chickamauga, his critical defense of Snodgrass House Hill prevented a Union disaster and gained him a recommendation for promotion to brigadier general. Harker saw further action at Chattanooga and Missionary Ridge, and led his brigade in the expedition to relieve General Ambrose E. Burnside's besieged force at Knoxville, Tennessee.

**Charles Garrison Harker
(John W. Kuhl)**

Colonel Harker was promoted to brigadier general on April 10, 1864, with a retroactive date of rank of September 20, 1863, the day he distinguished himself at Chickamauga. In the early stages of the Atlanta Campaign, Harker commanded the Third Brigade in the Fourth Corps' Second Division.

Kennesaw Mountain, 1864. (National Archives)

He was shot and mortally wounded while leading a charge at Kennesaw Mountain, Georgia, on June 27, 1864, and his remains were returned to Swedesboro for a full and honorable military burial. Tennessee historian Sam Elliott has characterized Harker as "one of the true heroes of the Army of the Cumberland." (Warner, *Generals in Blue*)

Richard Mendoza

Robert Harriot was born in Ireland in 1819, and began a "race performance" career at the age of fifteen. Harriot gained a reputation competing throughout the British Isles in walking and running competitions often featuring additional tasks like picking up stones, vaulting hurdles or walking a thin wooden plank. Monetary prizes were awarded and spectators gambled on the outcomes of these contests.

Robert Harriot in a pre-war "walking the plank" race. (*New York Clipper*)

Harriot immigrated to Jersey City in 1850 and continued as a professional "pedestrian," famed for walking "a thousand miles in a thousand hours." His carefree persona earned him the nickname "Mickey Free" after a character in the popular novel *Charles O'Malley: The Irish Dragoon*. In May 1852, Harriot married Eliza Fox in Newark. The couple had eight children. Eliza took up her husband's trade and became well known as a female competitor in the 1850s. "Mickey Free and Mrs. Free" were the only known performing "pedestrian couple."

In February 1861, when President-elect Lincoln visited Jersey City, Harriot, dressed as a "Wide Awake," or Republican activist, climbed the speakers' dais, shook Lincoln's hand, patted him on the back and was promptly clubbed off the platform by a policeman, much to the crowd's amusement. In August 1861, he enlisted in Company C of the 5th New Jersey Infantry, where his celebrity presence was noted by diarist **Alfred Bellard**. At the battle of Williamsburg in May 1862, Harriot lost several fingers to a shell fragment and during his convalescence in a Philadelphia hospital walked home to Jersey City for a visit. He was discharged for disability in February 1863, awarded a pension in April, and reenlisted as a private in Company B, 33rd New Jersey Infantry in August. Most of his service in the 33rd was as a hospital orderly and he was mustered out in July 1865.

A civilian again, Harriot returned to New Jersey to continue his career, albeit briefly and with limited success, as age and military service took a toll on his body. He became a mason and stonecutter and later Jersey City dog pound master, and built a "home on wheels," which he relocated around the city periodically. Always a colorful character, Harriot had several run-ins with the law, including charges of shooting at his wife and perjury. Robert "Mickey Free" Harriot died November 21, 1878, of pneumonia and is buried in Holy Name Cemetery, Jersey City. (Cumming, *Runners and Walkers*; *NY Clipper*; *NY Times*)

James M. Madden

Daniel Hart was born in 1839 in Phillipsburg, New Jersey, and in 1861 was employed as a clerk for a West Easton, Pennsylvania, merchant. In September, Hart enlisted as a second lieutenant in Company E, 7th New Jersey Infantry. A competent officer, he was promoted to first lieutenant in February 1862, and captain the following November.

Ellen & Daniel Hart (James M. Madden)

Captain Hart became a nationally known figure when the April 4, 1863, edition of *Harper's Weekly* published artist Alfred R. Waud's sketch of his March 12 wedding to Ellen "Nellie" Lammond in the 7th's winter quarters camp near Falmouth, Virginia. The ceremony became a grand social event attended by high-ranking officers including Generals Hooker, **Birney**, Ward, Carr and **Mott**, who all signed the marriage certificate as witnesses, and proved a morale booster for the Army of the Potomac following the disastrous Fredericksburg defeat of the previous December.

Hart was severely wounded while serving with his regiment at Chancellorsville in May 1863, and again at Spotsylvania in May 1864. While convalescing at military hospitals in Washington, he was nursed by Nellie and eventually returned to duty. Hart was promoted to major and lieutenant colonel of the 7th in 1865, and was awarded brevet ranks for gallant and meritorious service at Gettysburg and the battle of the Wilderness.

At the close of the war, Hart returned to Phillipsburg, where he operated a general store until 1867, when he joined the regular army as a first lieutenant in the African-American "Buffalo Soldier" 40th US Infantry regiment. When the African-American regiments were reorganized in 1869, Hart was transferred to Company G of the 25th Infantry and in 1873 was promoted to its captain. He served as commanding officer at Fort Quitman and later Fort Stockton, Texas, where Nellie gave birth to a son, Harry, in January 1876. Unfortunately, Captain Hart died of chronic malaria on April 11, 1878. He was buried at Fort Stockton Cemetery and his remains later reinterred in the San Antonio Texas National Cemetery.

Shortly after Hart's death, his widow was romantically linked to a philandering Fort Stockton captain who was court-martialed for accusing a fellow officer of "ungentlemanly acts." She subsequently moved to Washington with her son and died on September 4 1894. (Barnett, *Ungentlemanly Acts*; Madden & McGovern, "A Wedding in Camp")

James M. Madden

Llewellyn Frost Haskell was born on October 8, 1842, in Belleville, New Jersey, the son of wealthy pharmaceutical supplier Llewellyn Haskell. In the late 1850s, the elder Haskell created Llewellyn Park, the first planned community for wealthy people in the United States, in Orange (today's West Orange). Young Haskell was educated at **Rebecca Buffum Spring**'s progressive Eagleswood School in Perth Amboy from 1856 to 1860, and then attended the University of Heidelberg in Germany. When the Civil War broke out, he returned to the United States and enlisted as a private in the 84th New York Infantry (14th Brooklyn). In August 1861,

Llewellyn Frost Haskell (John W. Kuhl)

Haskell was commissioned as a lieutenant in the 5th Missouri Infantry and then transferred to the 27th Missouri Infantry. He served on the staff of General Alexander S. Asboth at the battle of Pea Ridge in early 1862, and then returned to the east as an aide to General Henry Prince. While on Prince's staff, he was severely wounded at the August 1862 battle of Cedar Mountain, Virginia.

Haskell was promoted to lieutenant colonel of the 7th United States Colored Infantry in October 1863. After serving with that African-American regiment in South Carolina and Virginia, he became colonel of the 41st United States Colored Infantry, a regiment organized in Philadelphia in November 1864 with 254 black Jerseymen in its ranks. In late March 1865, the 41st, as part of the Twenty-fifth Corps, played a role in the Union army's final assault on the Richmond – Petersburg line. Following the collapse of the Confederate defenses on April 2, the regiment joined in the pursuit of the defeated enemy, first along the South Side Railroad and then on to Appomattox Court House, where the 41st was present at the surrender of General Robert E. Lee's Army of Northern Virginia. Haskell was brevetted brigadier general on March 13, 1865, for his courageous and meritorious service in the war, and moved on to occupation duty in Texas with his men. The 41st was officially mustered out of service at Brownsville on September 30 and returned to Philadelphia.

After the war, Llewellyn Haskell worked with his father in the further development of Llewellyn Park. In 1877, he moved to San Francisco, where he was engaged in the furniture-manufacturing, mining and petroleum businesses. Haskell died at San Rafael, California, on November 26, 1929. (Bilby, *Forgotten Warriors*; Marquis, *Who's Who in America*)

Sylvia Mogerman

Clinton Pierson Heath was born into slavery on October 17, 1856, in New Bern, North Carolina. Slaves learning to read and write, as well as those who taught them how, were subject to severe penalties. According to family tradition, however, Heath's brother Calvin, taught by the sister of a plantation owner, then instructed Clinton and others despite the risk. Calvin wrote lessons surreptitiously in sand and if an overseer or master approached, his students erased the evidence by moving their feet in a shuffling movement resembling a dance.

Clinton Pierson Heath (Walter Spradley)

New Bern was captured by a Union force that included the 9th New Jersey Infantry in early 1862, and Union victory in the Civil War freed young Heath, who eventually became a farmer, an occupation for which he apparently had a natural talent. In 1885, Heath met Edwin Beekman of Middletown, New Jersey, who was visiting North Carolina and always in search of employees for his sprawling Monmouth County farm. Beekman was impressed by the Heath brothers and offered both jobs, which they accepted.

After saving some money, Clinton sent south for his wife, Mary, and in 1890 the Heaths left the Beekman Farm. Calvin became the first preacher at the A.M.E. Zion Church on Red Hill Road, while Clinton went to work for the New York and Long Branch Railroad. After a stint as a section hand, he was promoted to Middletown railroad crossing flagman, and worked for the railroad for 42 years while remaining a part-time farmer.

Heath invested some of his earnings in real estate and at one point owned fifty acres near the intersection of Harmony Road and Route 35. His original farm is still maintained by the family and serves as a museum and learning center. The museum highlights Middletown's agrarian past and also holds the remaining collection of the "Old Spy House" museum. Clinton Pierson Heath died on June 25, 1936, at the age of 79 from injuries sustained in an auto accident. He is interred at his brother's church graveyard on Red Hill Road. The Monmouth County park system features a display on the Heath family's history and accomplishments at its Tatum Park location on Red Hill Road. (Heath Farm & Learning Center, 219 Harmony Road, Middletown,NJ; http://heathfarm.tripod.com/peacelane/; interview with Walter Spradley)

Thomas R. Burke Jr.

George Washington Helme was born in Kingston, Pennsylvania, in 1822. In the 1840s, Helme joined his brother Samuel in Louisiana, where he studied law, was admitted to the bar in 1851 and opened a law office in New Orleans. In 1858, Helme married Margaret Appleby of Spotswood, New Jersey.

Although Helme's first two children were born in New Jersey, he returned to Louisiana before the Civil War. In March 1862, he joined the Confederate army as captain of the Crescent Militia Regiment's Company G. The unit was engaged in heavy fighting at Shiloh, where Captain Helme's commander cited him for "coolness and bravery." In early June, the regiment's ninety-day enlistment expired and most of its men transferred to the 18th Louisiana Infantry.

On September 27, 1864, General Kirby Smith appointed Helme executive officer of the "iron works" in the Trans-Mississippi Department, where he was stationed at Marshall, Texas, and served in the Niter and Mining Corps under

George Washington Helme
(Jamesburg Historical Society)

special instructions from the chief of the ordnance bureau. According to family tradition, he was promoted to major during this period. In some postwar biographies he is referred to as a major general, but this rank appears to have been in error or, not uncommon for the era, imaginary.

At the close of the war, Helme immediately headed back to New Jersey and entered the real estate business. In 1872, in partnership with his brother-in-law, he took over his father-in-law's snuff and chewing tobacco factory, later becoming sole owner of what became the George W. Helme Tobacco Company, second largest snuff producer in the country. In the 1880s, Helme purchased a tract of land previously known as Railroad Mills and renamed it Helmetta, after his daughter Antoinette, nicknamed Etta, where he constructed a new snuff mill and 105 homes for his employees. Helmetta seceded from East Brunswick and became a separate municipality in 1888. Helme died on June 13, 1893, of a heart attack while sitting on the porch of his High Street home. The *Camden Post* reported that 1500 people attended his funeral. He was buried in the Helme family mausoleum at Fernwood Cemetery in Jamesburg. The snuff business stayed in the Helme family until 1956 and closed in 1993. (Lurie & Mappen, *Encyclopedia of New Jersey*)

Thomas R. Burke Jr.

Charles Hewitt was born on December 18, 1824, in New York City, where he became a mathematics teacher and principal at Columbia Grammar and Preparatory School. Hewitt left education in 1845 to become bookkeeper for Peter Cooper's newly established Trenton Iron Works. Cooper's original factory was located in New York City but was relocated to Trenton, where water power from the Delaware River reduced expensive coal consumption. The Trenton Iron Works eventually covered three and a half acres along the Delaware. With fifty-eight furnaces, it produced huge amounts of iron for use in building and railroad construction and wire making. The works produced the first "I" beam made in the United States and supplied structural girders used to build New York's Cooper Union and the Capitol building in Washington.

Charles Hewitt
(Jersey City Free Public Library)

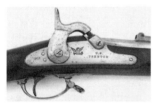

Model 1861 .58 caliber rifle-musket made in Trenton, NJ. (John W. Kuhl)

By 1861, Hewitt had become general manager of the Trenton Iron Works. In early 1862, he was contacted by Addison M. Burt and James T. Hodge, two New York entrepreneurs who had gained contracts to make 50,000 Model 1861 rifle-muskets and leased the Trenton Locomotive Works factory to produce them. Neither Burt nor Hodge had any experience in manufacturing firearms, so they spent the first half of 1862 buying machine tools and subcontracting parts orders, including to Trenton Iron Works, where Hewitt developed a process of rolling gun barrels for the Burt and Hodge project and other contractors. At the height of the war, the foundry could manufacture 1,000 gun barrels per week and also supplied both the Springfield and Watervliet arsenals with iron and gunmetal for ordnance production.

Hewitt eventually gained a significant interest in the Trenton Iron Works as well as in other Trenton businesses, including the New Jersey Steel & Iron Company, Trenton Water Power Company and the National Pottery Company. He also served on Trenton's Common Council and Board of Trade. In 1872, he was elected to the New Jersey State Senate, where he introduced legislation to create the Borough of Chambersburg. Charles Hewitt passed away on November 2, 1879, at his home in Chambersburg and is buried in Trenton's Mercer Cemetery. (Heroux & Mobray, *Civil War Arms Makers*; Raum, *History of the City of Trenton*)

Thomas R. Burke Jr.

Charles Fern Hopkins was born on May 16, 1842, in Hope, New Jersey. His father Nathan was a harness maker and Hopkins was apprenticed to that trade at the age of twelve. The senior Hopkins was also a fervent abolitionist, and his home was a station on New Jersey's Underground Railroad.

In June of 1861, Hopkins, by then a Boonton harness maker, enlisted in Company I of the 1st New Jersey Infantry. At Gaines' Mill, Virginia, on June 27, 1862, Hopkins was wounded twice. As the 1st retreated, he heard badly wounded Sergeant Richard Donnelly call out for help, halted and carried Donnelly to relative safety through a gauntlet of enemy fire. Wounded again himself, Hopkins collapsed on the field and was taken prisoner but paroled the following day. He was awarded the Medal of Honor for his selfless heroism in saving Donnelly, who survived to eventually become Quartermaster General of the New Jersey National Guard.

**Charles Fern Hopkins
(John W. Kuhl)**

Promoted to corporal, Hopkins was captured again in the battle of the Wilderness in May 1864. Less lucky this time, he ended up in the infamous Andersonville Prison. For ten months, Hopkins kept a diary of his suffering and privation, carefully recording the names of fellow Jerseymen who died in captivity. Eventually exchanged, he was mustered out of the army in Trenton in April 1865.

In 1867, Hopkins married Hettie Ann VanDuyne. The couple had seven children. A public-spirited citizen, he was elected mayor of Boonton in 1880 and also served as a New Jersey assemblyman, Morris County freeholder, State Senate assistant sergeant at arms and Boonton postmaster.

Hopkins spearheaded the effort to erect an Andersonville National Cemetery monument commemorating the 235 New Jersey soldiers and sailors who died there. The column, capped with the figure of a soldier at rest, reads: "Go, stranger, to New Jersey; tell her that we lie here in fulfillment of her mandate and our pledge, to maintain the proud name of our State, unsullied, and place it high on the Scroll of Honor, among the States of this Great Nation."

Charles F. Hopkins died on Feburary 14, 1934, the last surviving Civil War Medal of Honor recipient from New Jersey. He is buried in Greenwood Cemetery in Boonton. (Styple & Fitzpatrick, *Andersonville Diary*; Switala, *Underground Railroad*)

New Jersey Andersonville monument (New Jersey State Archives)

William B. Styple

Ellen Clementine Howarth was born Ellen Clementine Doran in Cooperstown, New York, on May 20, 1827. She left school at the age of seven to work in a factory and married Joseph Howarth, a calico printer like her father, in 1846. They had seven children. The Howarths moved to Trenton, New Jersey, where she began to write poems around the time of the Civil War. Howarth's work was printed in local newspapers under the name "Clementine" and then reprinted in magazines, gaining her a national following. She was a strong supporter of the Union and New Jersey's role in the Civil War. Her poem "My Jersey Blue," dedicated to the state's soldiers, was published in her book, *The Wind Harp, and Other Poems,* in 1864. "Clankings of the lion's chain" makes reference to British support for the Confederacy.

Oh! Who may know the strength, the treasure
Our country bleeds from every pore;
Or count the wasted lives, or measure
The fields made fertile with her gore?
And intervention and alliance,
Both clankings of the lion's chain,—
O for the power to bid defiance
To our insulting foe again!
When shall Columbia cease to smother
Her righteous ire? O, if we knew
We would rejoice my soldier brother!
Rejoice through all, my Jersey Blue!

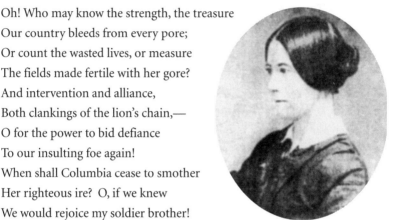

Ellen Clementine Howarth
(Women's Project of New Jersey)

Her second book, *Poems,* was published in 1868 in Newark. Howarth's best known poem is "Thou Wilt Never Grow Old." She was never able to make a living on her poetry and worked hard all her life, usually as a chair caner, to supplement her disabled husband's meager income. She always kept pencil and paper at hand, however, in case inspiration visited. Although no significant work followed *Poems,* Howarth's name commanded literary respect for a generation, and she was visited by former first lady Francis Folsom Cleveland on her birthday in 1899. According to her obituary, Howarth "said her poems came to her by inspiration while she worked about the house sweeping or at the washtub. She did not write them down at first, but kneaded them into shape in her brain and did not take up her pen until she was thoroughly satisfied with them. She began her output of verse without any preliminary study or training and after a period of great activity it suddenly ceased."

Ellen Clementine Howarth died in Trenton on December 23, 1899. (Lurie & Mappen, *Encyclopedia of New Jersey; NY Times* Obituary)

Joseph G. Bilby

Hugh Crowell Irish (Scott Hann)

Hugh Crowell Irish was born in Victory Township, New York, in 1832. At the age of sixteen, he apprenticed as a printer in Paterson, New Jersey, and after a period as a journeyman returned to Victory in 1854 to marry his childhood sweetheart, Betsey Ann Haight. The newlyweds moved to Paterson, where Irish became a partner at *The Guardian* newspaper and the couple had three children. Irish was active in local politics and became Paterson's tax assessor and clerk of the Passaic County Board of Chosen Freeholders. In 1862, he left the newspaper business and opened a grocery store – but not for long.

When New Jersey was assessed five new regiments for three-years service in the summer of 1862, Irish sold his grocery business and used the then empty store as a recruiting station, enlisting fifty-seven men in four days, which earned him the rank of captain of the 13th New Jersey Infantry's Company K. The 13th was organized and mustered into the service at Newark's Camp Frelinghuysen and entered combat at Antietam seventeen days after leaving the city.

At about 10:00 AM on September 17, 1862, with bullets zipping through the air around him, Captain Irish climbed a fence along the Hagerstown Pike. As he called out "Rally, boys, rally" to his troops, who had been badly shaken by heavy Confederate fire, he was shot through the chest and yelled, "I'm killed." The captain's lifeless body became entangled in the fence and was riddled by repeated hits. Captain Irish was the only New Jersey officer who died at Antietam. His body was retrieved from the field after the battle and returned to Paterson, where it was interred at Sandy Hill Baptist Cemetery, then moved to Cedar Lawn Cemetery in 1870.

Today, a bronze statue of Captain Irish, with sword drawn, stands atop the New Jersey monument at Antietam battlefield, dedicated in 1903. The Sons of Union Veterans honored the Captain by chartering their Hugh C. Irish Camp in Paterson. His sword and watch were presented to the Passaic County Historical Society and placed on display at Lambert Castle museum. During a museum renovation the relics associated with Captain Irish unfortunately vanished and have not been recovered to date. (Bilby & Goble, *Remember You Are Jerseymen*; Crowell, *The Young Volunteer*; Loewan, "The Captain and Mrs. Irish")

Norman Dykstra
Thomas R. Burke Jr.

Ellison Jamison was born in western Monmouth County in 1820 and became a farmer in the Cassville section of present-day Jackson Township. Jamison married Elizabeth Davis and together they had ten children. Elizabeth died with the birth of their last child in 1855 and in 1857 he married Etna Brown, with whom he would have another ten children. Most of New Jersey's Native Americans, the Lenni-Lenape, left the state in the 18th century, but family lore has it that Ellison's mother was of Native-American stock and that Etna Brown was of Lenape heritage as well.

Ellison Jamison (Thomas R. Burke, Jr.)

When Civil War broke out in 1861, two of Jamison's sons, William and Peter, enlisted into Company A of the 6th New Jersey Infantry. In July of 1862, the forty-two-year-old Jamison joined the federal army himself as a sergeant in Company F of the 14th New Jersey Infantry. Fate would not be kind to the Jamison family. Peter was killed at Williamsburg in 1862 and William was killed at Petersburg in 1864 while serving with the 8th New Jersey Infantry after reenlisting. Another son, Elwood, was luckier. He joined the 38th New Jersey Infantry in September 1864 and survived to be mustered out of service in June 1865.

Ellison Jamison suffered a head wound at the battle of Winchester on September 19, 1864, and later collapsed from heat stroke while marching across the Chain Bridge after the Army of the Potomac's Grand Review in Washington in May 1865. He was mustered out of the army while in the hospital recovering and returned home with a $2 a month disability pension. Jamison, who contributed more than his share to expanding the population base in today's southern Monmouth and northern Ocean counties, died in 1898 and is interred at the Cassville Methodist Cemetery in Jackson. (Martin, *The Monocacy Regiment*)

Thomas R. Burke Jr.

Joseph Kargé was born on July 4, 1823, in Posen, Poland, then part of Prussia. Kargé became a Prussian cavalry officer, but joined Polish revolutionaries and fled the country when their 1848 insurrection failed, immigrating to New York where he opened a small language school. In October 1861, Kargé was appointed lieutenant colonel of "Halsted's Horse," and when the unruly regiment became the 1st New Jersey Cavalry, his Prussian training techniques turned it into one of the best mounted units in the army. After the 1st's Colonel **Percy Wyndham** was captured at Harrisonburg, Virginia, in June 1862, Kargé led the regiment until he was badly wounded at Brandy Station, Virginia, in August.

Joseph Kargé (USAMHI/MOLLUS)

While convalescing in New Jersey during the Gettysburg Campaign, Kargé was ordered to raise two mounted regiments for thirty-days service. Although the emergency and need for troops quickly passed, he was then commissioned colonel of the 2nd New Jersey Cavalry. The 2nd was sent to the western theater, where Kargé matched wits with perhaps the best Confederate cavalry commander of the conflict, Nathan Bedford Forrest. In February 1864, Kargé and the 2nd successfully battled enemy horsemen near Okolona, Mississippi. Forrest responded by invading Tennessee with his entire force in March 1864 and Kargé, unfazed by the Rebel leader's aura of invincibility, defeated the Confederate cavalry at Bolivar, Tennessee, on May 2, handing Forrest his first loss of the war.

Kargé's reputation rose with his skillful handling of the Union rear guard after Forrest's victory at Brice's Cross Roads. As a brigade commander, he subsequently played a significant role in several important raids against Confederate supply lines in late 1864. In March 1865, Kargé's brigade took part in the campaign against Mobile, Alabama, which fell on April 12. In August 1865, he was brevetted to brigadier general of volunteers retroactive to March 13, 1865.

After the war, Kargé left the service and settled in Belleville, New Jersey. When civilian life proved too tame, he rejoined the army in 1867 but resigned four years later to become Professor of Continental Languages and Literature at Princeton. He was also much in demand on the lecture circuit. General Kargé died on December 27, 1892, of a heart attack while on a ferry crossing the Hudson River to New York City to visit his son. He is buried in Princeton Cemetery. (Kajencki, *Star on Many a Battlefield*)

Dr. David G. Martin

Philip Kearny (New Jersey State Archives)

Philip Kearny was born in New York City on June 1, 1815, spent his early years on a family estate near Newark and enlisted as a second lieutenant in the 1st U. S. Dragoons in 1836. In 1840, he was selected to study tactics at the French Cavalry School at Saumur, and while there accompanied the *Chasseurs d'Afrique* on a campaign against Algerian tribesmen.

During the Mexican War, Kearny, then a captain, was severely wounded leading an attack at Cherubusco, losing his left arm and gaining a brevet promotion to major. Remaining in the army despite disability, he campaigned against Indians in California and Oregon before resigning in 1851. Independently wealthy, Kearny moved to Paris and served as a volunteer in the French Imperial Guard Cavalry in the 1859 Italian Campaign. His heroism at the battle of Solferino earned him the distinction of being the first American soldier awarded the Legion of Honor

After the attack on Fort Sumter, Kearny returned to America and command of the 1st New Jersey Brigade. Longtime admirer Abraham Lincoln said of him: "Kearny is my brigadier, and no one shall be placed above him." General Kearny turned his raw troops into the finest volunteer brigade in the Army of the Potomac, refusing division command to remain with his beloved Jersey boys until directly ordered to it by General McClellan during the 1862 siege of Yorktown. He was promoted to major general on July 4, 1862.

Kearny fought at Williamsburg and Seven Pines, up to the gates of Richmond, then back down the Peninsula in the Seven Days fighting and again at Second Manassas. Entire companies of Rebel infantry were ordered to shoot "the One-Armed Devil" on sight. On September 1, 1862, at Chantilly, Virginia, he rode into an enemy picket line, was called on to surrender, attempted to escape and was killed. Kearny was buried in New York's Trinity Churchyard and in 1912 was reinterred at Arlington National Cemetery, where the state erected a bronze equestrian statue over his grave, bearing the words "New Jersey honors her most distinguished soldier" on its base.

Kearny's old brigade, once 4,000 strong, held its final reunion in 1925. Not wishing to "fade away," the fifteen survivors declared themselves disbanded with the words: "We're all close to death, let's march toward it in a body, the way Kearny used to, with a smile on his lips." (Styple, *Civil War Letters*)

William B. Styple

Hugh Judson Kilpatrick was born on January 14, 1836, near Deckertown, New Jersey. Kilpatrick graduated in 1861 from West Point, where he dropped his first name and excelled at public speaking. As a captain in the 5th New York Infantry, he was struck by a canister shot at the battle of Big Bethel in June 1861, becoming the first regular army officer wounded in the Civil War.

Promotions came fast to Kilpatrick. In September, he became lieutenant colonel of the 2nd New York Cavalry, and by the Gettysburg Campaign was a brigadier general commanding a division. After sparring with General J. E. B. Stuart's Southern horsemen prior to the battle, his command ended up on the federal left flank on July 3, 1863. Kilpatrick ordered Brigadier General Elon

Hugh Judson Kilpatrick (John W. Kuhl)

Farnsworth to lead his brigade across wooded terrain against Confederate infantry in an attack that shattered the brigade, killed Farnsworth and accomplished nothing.

The Farnsworth fiasco and other reckless decisions earned Kilpatrick the nickname "Kill-cavalry." His critics, then and later, alleged with some justification that he was a pint-sized egomaniacal dandy with flexible personal morals who gained advancement through political maneuvering and needlessly sacrificing his men. No one ever accused him of cowardice or a lack of combativeness, however.

In early 1864, Kilpatrick concocted a scheme to raid Richmond, free Union prisoners and capture the Confederate government. As Kilpatrick's division pushed south, his subordinate, Colonel Ulrich Dahlgren, led part of the force off on a secret mission. Poor coordination, bad weather and worse luck brought disaster. Dahlgren was killed, and papers discovered on his body indicated he had orders to assassinate Jefferson Davis, creating a flurry of allegations and denials.

Following the Richmond disaster, Kilpatrick went west to command a cavalry division under General W. T. Sherman. During the March to the Sea, he was apparently accompanied by a young woman dressed as a soldier, and it was reported that a Confederate raid on his camp flushed a scantily clad female from his quarters.

Following the war, Kilpatrick entered elective politics with little success, but he conducted a huge GAR veteran reunion on his Deckertown farm in 1878. He served as minister to Chile twice and died there on December 4, 1881, of kidney failure. He was buried at West Point. (Lurie & Mappen, *Encyclopedia of New Jersey;* Martin, *Kill-Cavalry*)

Thomas R. Burke Jr.

John Henry Lawson was born in Philadelphia on June 16, 1837, and enlisted in the Union navy during the Civil War. Although Lawson was an African-American, the navy was not segregated as the army was, and he was assigned to the crew of the *U.S.S. Hartford*, Admiral David Farragut's flagship.

During the August 5, 1864, battle of Mobile Bay, Lawson, serving in the rank of "landsman," equivalent to an army private, was part of a six-man team resupplying the *Hartford*'s big guns with ammunition. When an exploding enemy shell killed his comrades, Lawson disregarded his own wound and continued to participate in the fight as a gun crewman. For his actions that day he was awarded the Medal of Honor.

John Henry Lawson, (Library of Congress)

John Lawson's ship, the *Hartford*, engages the Confederate *Tennessee* at Mobile Bay. (*Harper's Weekly*)

Lawson's Medal of Honor citation reads: "On board the flagship U.S.S. *Hartford* during successful attacks against Fort Morgan, rebel gunboats and the ram *Tennessee* in Mobile Bay on 5 August 1864. Wounded in the leg and thrown violently against the side of the ship when an enemy shell killed or wounded the 6-man crew as the shell whipped on the berth deck, Lawson, upon regaining his composure, promptly returned to his station and, although urged to go below for treatment, steadfastly continued his duties throughout the remainder of the action."

Following the war, John Lawson returned to Philadelphia, and resided in the Philadelphia-Camden area for the rest of his life. A self-employed huckster, he had a large family, and many of his descendents still live in the area. Lawson died on May 3, 1919, and was buried at Mount Peace Cemetery, then in Center Township, now Lawnside, New Jersey. Although his gravestone crumbled over the years, and cemetery records were lost, Lawson's gravesite, along with those of more than 70 other African-American Civil War veterans buried in "Soldiers' Row" at Mount Peace, was rededicated on April 24, 2004.
(http://www.dvrbs.com/cw/CamdenCountyHeroes-JohnLawson.htm ; Bilby, *Forgotten Warriors*)

Joseph G. Bilby

Patrick Lynch was born in Ireland in 1846 and immigrated to the United States in 1859, settling in Newark. Lynch was an apprentice tinsmith by trade. The Panic of 1857 had depressed the job market in the city considerably, but he did find work and also served as a volunteer fireman. When the

Post-Civil War horse-drawn fire engine, Newark, NJ. (Newark Fire History)

Civil War broke out in 1861, many of Lynch's fellow firemen joined the army, but he was too young to volunteer. In April 1865, however, Lynch enlisted in Company E of the 9th New Jersey Volunteers, then driving inland towards Goldsboro, North Carolina. Although General Lee had surrendered in Virginia by the time Lynch reported for duty with his regiment, the situation in North Carolina was still unstable and the Confederates had only recently evacuated Goldsboro. The impending arrival of General Sherman's army of rowdy "bummers," whose reputation as looters and arsonists preceded them, led the town's grateful mayor and citizens to gladly surrender to the well-disciplined Jersey boys, who patrolled the streets and maintained order.

Dedication of 9th New Jersey monument at New Bern, 1905. (New Jersey State Archives)

The war in North Carolina ended conclusively a few weeks later and Lynch was discharged on July 12, 1865. He purchased his Springfield rifle-musket as a souvenir of his time in service, and the gun remains in the family's possession to this day. After the war, Lynch returned to Newark, where he married in 1870 and resumed his service with the city's fire department. He became a full-time professional fireman assigned to Hook & Ladder #3, a first-class, horse-drawn engine. Lynch also became very active in veterans' affairs and was involved in the placement of a monument to his old regiment at New Bern, North Carolina, in 1905. On retirement, he was granted exempt fireman status and at the time of his death on January 20, 1921, Patrick Lynch was the longest tenured fireman in Newark Fire Department history. He was buried in the "Soldier's Field" section of Newark's Holy Sepulchre Cemetery. (Bilby & Goble, *Remember You Are Jerseymen*; Scully family interview)

Thomas R. Burke Jr.

Robert McAllister (New Jersey State Archives)

Robert McAllister was born in Juniata County, Pennsylvania, on June 1, 1813. McAllister, a supervisor of railroad construction crews, moved to Oxford Furnace, New Jersey, in 1857 to construct a railroad tunnel. His experience as a militia officer in both Pennsylvania and New York led him to raise a company of volunteers at the beginning of the Civil War and gained him a commission as lieutenant colonel of the 1st New Jersey Infantry. McAllister led the regiment during the Peninsula Campaign and the bloody battle of Gaines' Mill on June 27, 1862. In August, he was promoted to colonel and assigned to command of the newly raised 11th New Jersey Infantry. The 11th was heavily engaged at Chancellorsville and was badly shot up on the second day at Gettysburg, where McAllister was severely wounded twice, by a spherical case-shot ball in his left thigh and a shell fragment in his right foot.

After returning from convalescent leave, McAllister was again wounded while leading the 11th at the Wilderness in May 1864. The next month he was given command of the Second Corps' Third Division's Third Brigade, which he led through the end of the war. McAllister's conduct in handling his brigade at the battle of Boydton Plank Road in October 1864 was highly praised and earned him the brevet rank of brigadier general. At the close of the war he was honored for his service with the rank of brevet major general. McAllister was mustered out of the military on June 6, 1865, after participating in forty-one fights from Bull Run to Appomattox. The only major battles in the northern Virginia theater of war that he missed were South Mountain and Antietam, when his command was held in reserve near Washington, DC. After the war, McAllister lived in Belvidere, NJ, where he became manager of the Ironton Railroad Company. He suffered a stroke in 1887 and died on February 23, 1891. He was buried in Belvidere Cemetery.

General McAllister wrote over 900 letters home during the war. They were edited for publication in 1965 by James I. Robertson, Jr., and clearly demonstrate his serious attitude and religious outlook on life. He was an able and sincere officer who carried out his duties well without grandstanding. His troops called him "Mother McAllister" because of his personal habits and also because of his careful attention to their needs. (Robertson, *McAllister*)

Dr. David G. Martin

George Brinton McClellan was born in Philadelphia on December 3, 1826, the son of a prominent physician and founder of Jefferson Medical College. He graduated second in his class from West Point in 1846 and was commissioned a second lieutenant in the engineer corps. McClellan served in the Mexican War, was promoted to captain, appointed an instructor at West Point and assigned as an official American observer of the Crimean War. His observations abroad led him to design the McClellan saddle, which, in various versions, has remained the official army saddle since 1859. McClellan resigned his commission in 1857 to become a railroad executive.

George Brinton McClellan
(National Archives)

McClellan reentered military service following the outbreak of the Civil War. Commissioned a major general in May 1861, he was successful in a minor campaign in the west and then named to command of the Military Division of the Potomac and, for a while, the entire Union army. A great organizer, McClellan created the Army of the Potomac out of a milling post-Bull Run near rabble. He became immensely popular with his troops, but less so with the country's political leadership, as his dilatory campaigning, evidenced in the Peninsula battles of 1862 and the aftermath of Antietam, frustrated Abraham Lincoln, who eventually relieved him from command. On November 5, 1862, McClellan was ordered to Trenton to "await orders," which never came.

The Democratic nominee for president in 1864, McClellan was defeated by Lincoln but captured the electoral vote of his new home state. After the Civil War, he moved to Orange (today's West Orange) and in 1877 was nominated by the Democrats for governor of New Jersey. Still popular in the state, McClellan won in a landslide. As governor from 1878 to 1881, he generally supported consensus causes like reducing tax rates, government support of education and nascent industries, and enhancement of the National Guard, but got little substantive done. He displayed increasingly diminished interest in his office, remarking that it was "a nuisance to be obliged to go to Trenton."

General McClellan died at his Orange estate on October 29, 1885, and is buried at Riverview Cemetery in Trenton, under the tallest monument in the cemetery. His self-exculpatory autobiography was posthumously published in 1887. McClellan's home, "Maywood," is now part of the Seton Hall Preparatory School campus in West Orange. (Lurie & Mappen, *Encyclopedia of New Jersey*; Sears, *Young Napoleon*; Stellhorn & Birkner, *Governors of New Jersey*)

Thomas R. Burke Jr.
Dr. David G. Martin

William Henry "Willie" McGee was born on May 13, 1849, in Newark, New Jersey, the son of Irish immigrants. In 1855, McGee's father disappeared or died, breaking up the family. In 1860, Willie was living with an aunt and uncle in Newark.

William Henry "Wille" McGee's Newark. The corner of Broad and Market Streets in 1865. (*Short History of Newark*)

On August 29, 1863, McGee left his job as a waiter to enlist in the 33rd New Jersey Infantry's Company C as a musician. He appears to have campaigned with the regiment through January 1864, then was supposedly hospitalized with typhoid. With the assistance of Chaplain Holmes Pattison, McGee was appointed a hospital orderly when the 33rd marched off on the Atlanta Campaign. In December 1864, serving as a mounted orderly during a small battle in the Nashville Campaign, McGee reportedly rallied two regiments and led them to capture enemy artillery and several hundred prisoners. He rejoined the 33rd in Washington in June 1865, was discharged, returned to Newark, but then moved to Michigan and was adopted by Pattison. In 1866, he was awarded the Medal of Honor for his actions in December 1864.

McGee's postwar tale is bizarre, marking him as one of New Jersey's greatest con men. Using Pattison as his mentor, he convinced Governor **Marcus Ward** to hire tutors to help him pass a test to become an army officer, then, in a drunken rage, shot and killed another officer and was sentenced to prison. Once released, McGee used Ward to gain a presidential pardon, then pawned his Medal of Honor and panhandled money from Ward to retrieve it. He married three different women and deserted them, joined the 7th US Cavalry as an enlisted man and later passed himself off as the only survivor of Custer's Last Stand.

In 1878, after a stint as a hobo, McGee applied for a disability pension based on nonexistent war wounds, a process that revealed his 1864 heroics as entirely fabricated. He then convinced a congressman to introduce a bill granting him back pay and reinstatement as an officer. It failed, but at one point he had convinced Lizzie Borden's lawyer to go to bat for him. The McGee saga ended in New York City in 1904, when Willie stabbed a man to death in a fight over a meat pie. Sentenced to Sing Sing, McGee was denied an appeal for clemency. Prison records from the era no longer exist, so his final fate and resting place are unknown. (Fox, *Drummer Boy Willie McGee*)

Thomas Fox
Joseph G. Bilby

"The First Shot" fired at the *Star of the West*, January 9, 1861. (*Harper's Weekly*)

John McGowan was born in Philadelphia, Pennsylvania, on December 3, 1805. He took to the sea at age 13 and at 25 was appointed an officer of the United States Revenue Marine Service (forerunner of the Coast Guard), serving during the Seminole Indian War and the Mexican War. In 1849, then Lieutenant McGowan was detailed to establish life-saving "boathouses" on the New Jersey coast between Little Egg Harbor and Cape May. In 1853, shortly after being promoted to captain, he resigned to enter civilian life as a commander of merchant steamships and moved his family to Elizabeth, New Jersey.

Following the secession of South Carolina from the Union in December 1860, federal troops occupying Fort Sumter in Charleston Harbor refused to surrender the post to state authorities. The situation led to a standoff between the federal government under lame-duck President James Buchanan and the rebellious government of South Carolina. On January 5, 1861, Buchanan dispatched the merchant steamer *Star of the West,* under McGowan's command, from New York on a mission to resupply Fort Sumter. When Captain McGowan attempted to approach the fort in the early morning hours of January 9, with his ship prominently displaying the United States flag, a South Carolina battery manned by Citadel cadets based on Morris Island fired a shot across his bow, followed by two rounds which actually hit the *Star of the West*. McGowan, whose vessel was unarmed, aborted the mission and returned to New York. Historians commonly consider this engagement to be the South's first openly hostile fire against the Union.

On August 12, 1861, McGowan rejoined the Revenue Marine at his old rank and served throughout the remainder of the Civil War, organizing the "Mosquito Fleet," which patrolled and blockaded Chesapeake Bay. His wife, Catherine Caldwell McGowan, decorated their Elizabeth home with red, white and blue bunting at every Union victory, and his son John entered the navy, retiring as an admiral in 1901. In the postwar era, the elder McGowan was again made responsible for constructing life-saving stations along the coast prior to retiring. He died at his longtime home in Elizabeth on January 18, 1891, and was buried in nearby Evergreen Cemetery in Hillside. (Detzer, *Allegiance*; *NY Times* Obituaries)

Steven D. Glazer

Elias Joseph Marsh was born in Paterson, New Jersey, in 1835, the son of a physician of the same name. Marsh graduated from New York's Columbia College of Physicians and Surgeons in 1858, and then, seeking adventure, traveled to Saint Louis, Missouri, where he became a ship's doctor on an American Fur Company Missouri River steamer. His detailed diary of a frontier voyage up the Missouri was subsequently published. Marsh eventually returned to Paterson and enlisted in the 3rd New Jersey Militia as an assistant surgeon in April 1861. Following this three-month enlistment, he was commissioned in the United States Army Volunteer Medical Corps and served in the Peninsula Campaign.

Elias Joseph Marsh (John W. Kuhl)

Marsh subsequently served as director of Judiciary Hospital in Washington for nine months, and at the end of the war was a cavalry brigade surgeon. An undocumented but possible story related in his obituary placed Marsh at Appomattox, where Generals Grant and Lee were meeting to arrange Lee's surrender, and from where, having a fresh horse, he reportedly carried Grant's cease-fire order to a number of regiments, gaining a reputation as "The Man Who Stopped the War." Marsh remained in the army after the war and served with General Philip Sheridan's army of occupation in Texas. He was later assigned to duties in California and as medical director of the United States Military Academy at West Point.

In 1870, Marsh left the army and returned to New Jersey, where he married, had four children, resumed the practice of civilian medicine and eventually became president of the Medical Society of New Jersey. On retiring from private practice, he worked for the Metropolitan Life Insurance Company and developed longevity prediction tables that were used by the company well into the next century. His research work was so well regarded that he was awarded a gold medal at a Paris Exposition. Doctor Marsh died on August 3, 1901, and is buried at Cedar Lawn Cemetery in Paterson in the Marsh family plot. (http://www.civilwarsurgeonsmemorial.org/)

Valerie M. Josephson

Levi DeWitt Miller was born to Peter and Margaret Smith Miller on February 22, 1836, in Harmony, New Jersey. Miller attended and graduated from Belvidere Academy and trained for a year with his older brother John, a prominent Andover physician, then attended and graduated from the College of Physicians and Surgeons in New York in 1855. He established a medical practice in Lafayette and in August 1862 was commissioned assistant surgeon in the 1st New Jersey Infantry, a regiment in service since 1861.

Levi DeWitt Miller (John W. Kuhl)

In March 1864, after conducting physical examinations of recent recruits, Miller became enraged over the quality of men the state was forwarding to his unit and registered his anger in a letter to the *Sussex Register*. Miller wrote that one new soldier, who had previously received a disability discharge for "epileosia, variocele, [and] organic disease of the heart," had been allowed to reenlist even though his "left arm was powerless due to a disunited fracture of both bones of the forearm of six months standing, and which he carries in a sling." He went on to assert that recruiters were committing fraud for profit and that the recruit had criminal intent as well, since he would be paid an enlistment bounty while knowing full well he could not serve. The town whose quota he helped fill would also benefit, but the army would suffer. Miller's observations were sustained by other surgeons and officers, and brigade commander Colonel William Penrose convened a board to review the matter and report to Governor **Joel Parker**.

Miller resigned his commission in June 1864 and moved to New York City, where he opened an office and pharmacy. He returned to New Jersey in 1868, opened a practice in Newton, and married Mary E. Cummins of Lafayette on September 30. The couple had two sons. Doctor Miller was an involved citizen. After an 1873 Main Street fire that caused $65,000 worth of damage, Miller and other prominent residents formed a committee and voted to purchase a modern "steamer" fire engine. The $5000 engine arrived in October 1873 and in a highly attended public trial projected water 265 feet through 150 feet of hose. Miller died on July 21, 1895, of cardiac disease and is buried in the Old Newton Cemetery not far from where he lived. (http://www.civilwarsurgeonsmemorial.org/; Bilby & Goble, *Remember you are Jerseymen*)

Valerie M. Josephson

George Washington Mindil was born in Frankfort, Germany, in 1843, immigrating to Philadelphia with his family six years later. In 1861, Mindil joined the 23rd Pennsylvania Infantry as a second lieutenant and was promoted to captain. During the Peninsula Campaign, he served as a staff officer in the Third Army Corps, was awarded the Medal of Honor for "distinguished bravery" at the battle of Williamsburg and gained a place on General **Philip Kearny**'s staff.

When Kearny was killed, Mindil was left without a position, but the connection proved fortuitous in the fall of 1862, when the 27th New Jersey Infantry was organized in Newark. The regiment was technically part of the state militia, so officers had the right to elect their colonel. When prominent politician and Kearny friend **Cortlandt Parker**

George Washington Mindil
(John W. Kuhl)

recommended Mindil, the nineteen-year-old was elected unanimously. Mindil, the youngest man to serve as a New Jersey colonel, commanded the 27th throughout its nine-months service, which ended during the Gettysburg Campaign. He offered to extend the regiment's tour of duty during the emergency and was awarded another Medal of Honor for that "action." The second award was one of a number dubiously granted at this time due to legislative loopholes in the medal's original authorization. All, including Mindil's, were rescinded in 1916.

On returning to New Jersey in the summer of 1863, Mindil was appointed colonel of the newly formed 33rd New Jersey Infantry. He commanded the 33rd during its service in the west, which included the battles for Chattanooga, the Atlanta Campaign, the March to the Sea and the Carolinas Campaigns. During part of that period, Mindil was acting brigade commander and also missed some time due to illness and injury. He was promoted to brevet major general at the end of the war.

In 1895, Mindil was appointed to the position of examiner of jewelry and precious stones for the Port of New York. He was removed in 1907 under charges of corrupt collusion with a jewelry importer and unfortunately died on July 20, 1907, shortly before completion of an investigation that might have cleared his name. Ironically, his death occurred on the forty-third anniversary of the battle of Peach Tree Creek, where the 33rd suffered its worst losses of the war. Some of Mindil's papers are in the collections of the New Jersey Historical Society. (Zinn, *The Mutinous Regiment*)

John Zinn

26th New Jersey Veteran Reunion Badges.
(John W. Kuhl)

David T. Morrill was born on October 24, 1825, in Danville, Vermont. He was ordained to the Baptist ministry in 1854 and almost immediately accepted a call to be pastor of the Fifth Baptist Church in Newark's East Ward. In the late summer of 1862, Morrill encouraged enlistment in the 26th New Jersey Infantry, a nine-month service regiment raised in Newark, Orange, South Orange, Bloomfield and Caldwell, and dubbed "The Flower of Essex County." The unit was mustered in on September 18 at Newark's Camp Frelinghuysen, located on a field between the Morris Canal and Roseville Avenue, and left for Washington shortly afterward. Morrill himself joined the regiment as chaplain in October.

Reverend Morrill's military experience proved very disillusioning, leading him to complain about Sunday marches, shirkers, "homebound patriots," red tape, and especially incompetent leadership. Although his was probably far from a unique experience, as a correspondent to the *Newark Daily Advertiser*, Morrill had a unique platform to express his frustrations. He took full advantage of that opportunity, writing almost forty letters to the Newark paper. Criticized for his comments, Morrill responded: "It is one thing to say how the army ought to feel and another to say how it does feel." For his part, Morrill said, "I mean to state what is." Frustration with Morrill's candor reached the point that special orders were issued in June of 1863 dismissing him from his chaplain's position for correspondence that was both "unbecoming and disloyal." The orders did not reach Newark, however, until after Morrill had already left the army, as the 26th was mustered out that same month. When Morrill applied for a postwar pension, his dismissal orders were found to be invalid. After the war, Morrill moved to the midwest, serving Baptist churches in Missouri and Illinois. He died on October 9, 1893, in Belvidere, Illinois. (Siegel, *For the Glory of the Union*)

John Zinn

Andrew Jackson Morrison was born in Washington County, New York, on October 3, 1831. Discharged as an underage recruit in the Mexican War, he got to the front as an "aide" to a captain, then drifted to New Orleans and joined Cuban rebel Narcisco Lopez's ragtag army. Morrison never made it to Cuba, where Lopez was captured and shot. After failing to raise volunteers for Italian revolutionary Giuseppe Garibaldi, he ended up working at the New York City Customs Office.

In December 1855, Morrison signed on with mercenaries shipping out to join William Walker, the soldier of fortune conqueror of Nicaragua. The expedition ended abruptly

Andrew Jackson Morrison (USAMHI/MOLLUS)

when the U.S. Revenue Service arrested the hapless band of inebriated heroes and removed them, yelling, singing and manacled, from a ship to shore. Morrison eventually reached Nicaragua and served until Walker was overthrown in 1857. In 1860, he fought in Italy as a cavalry captain under Garibaldi.

The Civil War found Morrison back in America. After stints as colonel of a horseless New York cavalry unit and an aide in the Peninsula Campaign, he was elected colonel of the 26th New Jersey Infantry in September 1862. A popular commander fond of roaring campfires, fine whiskey and good cigars, Morrison led the 26th in its first battle, a snowball fight against a Vermont regiment. He was unhorsed and captured. In May 1863, during the battle of Second Fredericksburg, Morrison was ordered to lead his regiment against a Confederate position. Shouting incoherently, he rode off in the wrong direction. The regiment fell into chaos but was reorganized by Lieutenant Colonel Edward Martindale and completed its mission. Morrison was relieved from command, placed under arrest for drunkenness and cashiered from the army. Incredibly, in 1863 he convinced Governor **Joel Parker** to have his dismissal revoked and appoint him colonel of the 3rd New Jersey Cavalry. The 3rd left the state in April 1864 but failed to live up to expectations. Morrison, this time acquitted of conduct "unbecoming an Officer and a Gentleman," resigned for "reasons referring to the interests of the service and myself."

Colonel Morrison settled in West Troy, New York, where he became a railway postal agent, published his memoirs, *Fighting Under Three Flags*, and painted Italianate landscapes. When he died in 1907, his obituary noted that the colonel passed from this world "unburdened by wealth." (Bilby, "Through Hades;" Siegel, "*For the Glory of the Union*)

Joseph G. Bilby

Gershom Mott was born in Lamberton on April 7, 1822. Educated at the Trenton Academy, he served as a second lieutenant in the 10th U. S. Infantry in the Mexican War. He later married Elizabeth Smith and was a teller at the Bordentown bank when the Civil War began.

Mott became lieutenant colonel of the 5th New Jersey Infantry in August 1861, and was promoted to colonel of the 6th New Jersey Infantry in May 1862. Cited for coolness and courage at Williamsburg and at Second Bull Run, where he was wounded, he was promoted to brigadier general in September. On rejoining the army after Fredericksburg, Mott assumed command of the 2nd New Jersey Brigade. He was severely wounded again at Chancellorsville in May 1863, but he refused to leave his men until forced to do so from loss of blood. He did not return to the army until autumn.

Gershom Mott
(New Jersey State Archives)

In 1864, Mott commanded the Second Corps' Fourth Division. At Spotsylvania he was ordered to support an attack, but many of his men, their enlistments about to expire, refused to advance. When a staff officer reported that Mott appeared bewildered, he was relieved from command and his division was disbanded. Historian Gordon Rhea, however, concludes: "History has judged Mott unfairly. Grant and Meade asked him to perform an impossible task, gave him too few men to accomplish it, and sent him forward at the wrong time." Demoted to brigade command, he was restored to division command in July. Wounded just before the Confederate surrender at Appomattox, Mott received brevet promotion to major general, was promoted to full major general in May 1865, and resigned from the army in 1866.

Back in New Jersey, Mott became paymaster of the Camden and Amboy Railroad and major general in the New Jersey National Guard. In 1875, he was appointed New Jersey state treasurer and served as state prison warden from 1876 to 1881. In 1878, Mott was accused of torturing prisoners by gagging, paddling, using the "stretcher," and "dungeon" confinement. He admitted to being a "disciplinarian" but denied mistreatment and was exonerated of the charges. General Mott passed away in New York City on November 29, 1884, and was buried with full military honors at Trenton's Riverview Cemetery. Fort Mott in the Delaware River was named in his honor. (Lurie & Mappen, *Encyclopedia of New Jersey*; Rhea, *Spotsylvania Court House;* Sackett, *Modern Battles of Trenton*)

Thomas R. Burke Jr.
John W. Kuhl

Philip Muldoon was born in New York in September 1844 and moved to New Jersey three years later with his Irish-born widowed mother and two sisters. In August of 1862, when he enlisted as a private for a nine-month tour of duty with Company D of the 21st New Jersey Infantry in Hoboken, Muldoon was working as a boilermaker.

On May 4, 1863, the 21st was overrun by Confederates near Bank's Ford during the battle of Chancellorsville. The regiment's Colonel **Gilliam Van Houten** was mortally wounded and captured along with a number of his men, including Muldoon. Private Muldoon was paroled by his captors on May 13 and mustered out of service on June 19 at Trenton. On his return to New

Camp of the 21st New Jersey, Belle Plain, VA.
(James M. Madden)

Jersey and civilian life, he settled in Jersey City, married in 1870 and had six children. Muldoon later became a partner in the Kelly and Muldoon cigar store at the corner of Morgan and Grove Streets in Jersey City and also opened a millinery shop at 104 Newark Ave.

Along with his business interests, Muldoon became involved in local politics, and a back room in his cigar store became headquarters for Robert "Little Bob" Davis, a former plumber elected as a Jersey City alderman in 1885. The Irish-born Davis went on to become Hudson County sheriff and supervisor of the county jail, as well as a "consummate political boss" who ran the Hudson County Democratic Party as his fiefdom and seriously contested party control across the state. In the early twentieth century, Davis turned reformer and, before his death in 1911, backed Woodrow Wilson for governor. Muldoon rose alongside his friend and served as director of education and superintendent of sewers in Jersey City in the late nineteenth and early twentieth centuries. He and his wife Mary were also very active in veterans' affairs at the GAR Van Houten Post #3 and Relief Post #16 of the organization's Ladies' Auxiliary. Muldoon retired from all business and social activities due to illness in 1914 and died on July 22, two months after Mary. He was buried in Holy Name Cemetery, Jersey City. (Bilby, *Remember You Are Jerseymen*; Lurie & Mappen, *Encyclopedia of New Jersey*)

John Hallanan

Franklin Murphy was born in Jersey City on January 3, 1846, and his family subsequently moved to Newark. A Newark Academy student in 1862, he responded to President Lincoln's call for additional volunteers by enlisting in Colonel **Ezra A. Carman's** 13th New Jersey Infantry. The minimally trained regiment engaged in its first fight at Antietam in September 1862. Although a bullet tore through his forage cap, young Murphy miraculously escaped injury on what would be the bloodiest single day in American military history.

Franklin Murphy
(New Jersey Historical Society)

Following Antietam, the 13th guarded the Chesapeake & Ohio Canal, then established winter quarters near Stafford Court House, Virginia. In May 1863, the regiment fought at Chancellorsville, losing 130 men killed, wounded or missing. In July, the 13th was in action at Culp's Hill during the battle of Gettysburg, and in late September was sent west, subsequently serving at Chattanooga and in General William T. Sherman's Atlanta Campaign, March to the Sea and Carolinas Campaigns. Murphy rose to the rank of first lieutenant by February 1864, and his surviving diaries provide a gripping account of the 13th's war.

On his return to New Jersey, Murphy's father gave him a half interest in a Newark varnish company. He improved the product and sold enough of it to make him a wealthy man. From 1883 to 1886, Murphy was a member of Newark's Common Council. He also served as Essex County parks commissioner, a state assemblyman and trustee of the state Reform School. President McKinley appointed him a commissioner to the Paris Universal Exposition in 1900, and he held numerous financial, social, and civic positions.

Murphy chaired the Republican Party's state committee from 1892 to 1904 and again from 1907 to 1910, and was governor from 1902 to 1905. A moderate progressive, he improved child labor laws, instituted civil service reforms and oversaw the first of New Jersey's election primary laws. In 1902, he hosted President Theodore Roosevelt's visit to the New Jersey summer capital at Sea Girt.

Murphy was an unsuccessful candidate for the vice presidential nomination to run with William Howard Taft in 1908. He died in Palm Beach, Florida, on February 24, 1920, and is buried in Mount Pleasant Cemetery, Newark. There is a statue of him in the city's Weequahic Park. (Lurie & Mappen, *Encyclopedia of New Jersey,* Olsen, *A Billy Yank Governor*; Stellhorn & Birkner, *The Governors of New Jersey*)

Bernard A. Olsen
Thomas R. Burke Jr.

David Naar was born a Sephardic Jew in Saint Thomas, Virgin Islands, on November 10, 1800. Naar immigrated with his family to New York, and then moved to New Jersey in 1834, where he quickly became involved in Democratic Party politics, serving as mayor of Elizabeth and an Essex County judge. In 1853, Naar moved to Trenton and bought the *Trenton True American* newspaper. Although he editorially espoused progressive policies in the area of public education, Naar was an unapologetic racist who defended the institution of slavery in the South as embodying a natural racial social order.

David Naar (*New Jersey Jewish News*)

After the outbreak of war, Naar editorially attacked the Lincoln administration at every opportunity, and condemned the Emancipation Proclamation and the recruiting of black soldiers into the Union army. He was careful, however, to neither advocate a Confederate victory nor disparage New Jersey's troops in the field, making him, according to historian William Gillette, a "moderate copperhead"— at least publicly. A loyal Democrat, he enjoyed considerable public printing business during the administration of Governor **Joel Parker.**

Naar's editorial stances did not damage his postwar political career, and he served as state treasurer in 1865-1866 and Trenton Common Council member from 1869 to 1871. He retired from his editorial post at the *True American* in 1874 and died on February 24, 1880. (Gillette, *Jersey Blue;* Lurie & Mappen, *Encyclopedia of New Jersey*)

Joseph G. Bilby

Thomas Nast (Library of Congress)

Thomas Nast was born on September 27, 1840, in Landau, a small Bavarian town near the French border. Like many Germans, the Nast family immigrated to New York in 1846 to avoid political repression. Never a diligent student, Nast took a job as an illustrator at the age of fifteen as an alternative to school and soon excelled at wood engraving, which was used to illustrate newspapers and magazines before the printing of photographs became feasible.

Nast worked for many periodicals, but his depictions of the Civil War and political events for *Harper's Weekly* made him a household name. He traveled to the front, and his sketches portraying devastated battlefields, war-torn families, and the heroic struggles of Union troops struck a popular chord. Nast was the first artist to symbolically portray the Democratic donkey and Republican elephant, and also turned the image of "Uncle Sam" into a government figure used to promote patriotism. Nast's Civil War sketches became so iconic that Abraham Lincoln stated: "Nast has become our best recruiting sergeant. His emblematic cartoons have never failed to arouse enthusiasm and patriotism." Like many German-Americans, Nast was an ardent Republican and supporter of the Union.

It was during the Civil War that Nast created his first Christmas drawings to cheer up readers and raise their morale. Nast's image of "Santa Claus" became so popular that his representation remains the popular portrait still in use today, although without the Union army uniform Santa wore in 1862. His postwar drawings depicting the corrupt New York City politician "Boss" Tweed are credited with helping bring down Tweed's organization. Those depictions, as well as caricatures of Democratic presidential candidate Horace Greeley and Nast's anti-Catholic clergy cartoons, led to threats against the artist, which, along with a belief that the town's altitude would help cure recurring throat infections, led him to relocate to Morristown, New Jersey, in 1872. He lived in Morristown for the rest of his life.

On December 7, 1902, while serving as Theodore Roosevelt's consul general in Ecuador, Nast contracted yellow fever and died. His body was returned to America, where he was interred at Woodlawn Cemetery in the Bronx. Every December, Morristown holds a Thomas Nast Day featuring displays of his art and lectures on his role in American history and contributions to American popular culture. (Lurie & Mappen, *Encyclopedia of New Jersey*; Paine, *Thomas Nast*)

Lesley-Ann Thomson

Christoph Niederer was born on April 12, 1836, in Auerbach, Bavaria. Niederer immigrated to New York in 1853, became a cabinetmaker and enlisted as a private for two years service in the 20th New York Infantry's Company F in 1861. The regiment was recruited from German *Turnverein* fraternal, gymnastic and political clubs in the New York City area (one company came from Newark) and was known as the "Turner Rifles." After camping a month at Turtle Bay Brewery, the regiment headed south and fought at Cape Hatteras, on the Virginia Peninsula and at Antietam.

Christoph Niederer
(West Paterson *Herald News*)

Niederer was promoted to corporal in November 1862, and served with the 20th until April 1863, when he and 197 other noncommissioned officers and privates claimed their enlistments had expired, stacked arms and refused further duty. The army disagreed and ordered them back to duty. The stubborn Germans refused, were court-martialed for mutiny in the face of the enemy, found guilty, dishonorably discharged and sentenced to serve hard labor. The remainder of the regiment's men fought at Chancellorsville and returned home on May 7. Because of previous good behavior, the mutineers were discharged, albeit dishonorably, on August 15, 1863.

Niederer married Johanna Joachim in 1865. The couple moved to Carlstadt, New Jersey, in 1868, where they raised six children. Niederer played a significant role in preserving German-American cultural traditions in northern New Jersey as owner of the Mount Pleasant Park and Hotel, a combination beer and dance hall, bowling alley and rifle range in Carlstadt. He was also politically active in town, serving as a councilman and a founder of the local GAR post, which was organized in his home in 1878.

Niederer and his fellow mutineers claimed their 1863 dishonorable discharges were voided in 1866, but when they applied for veterans' pensions the government held the discharges valid and rejected their applications. It took a special act of Congress passed in 1905 to exonerate the men of the 20th New York by name and grant them the right to receive pensions.

Christoph Niederer left behind a detailed diary in German, which covered most of his wartime service. Many excerpts were published in the 1960s by the West Paterson *Herald News* to commemorate the Civil War Centennial. He died on March 2, 1909, and is buried in the Berry Lawn Cemetery in Carlstadt. (McAfee, "20th New York"; West Paterson *Herald News*)

Catherine Cassidy

Elizabeth Niles is buried in an unmarked grave next to her husband. (Robert Silverman & Diana Newman)

Elizabeth Niles, born in 1844, began married life with her husband Martin only three months before she allegedly passed herself off as a man and they both enlisted in the 14th Vermont Infantry in September 1862. According to later family revelations, Elizabeth, "with close cropped hair and a uniform," served alongside Martin under an assumed name and her true identity was never discovered. The 14th was part of a brigade of Vermonters enlisted for nine-months service that spent most of its military career on garrison duty in the defenses of Washington. The brigade was sent to reinforce the Army of the Potomac during the Gettysburg Campaign, however, and played a vital role in the repulse of Pickett's Charge on July 3, 1863, firing into the right flank of the advancing Confederate force and hastening its collapse.

After returning to civilian life, Martin and Elizabeth settled in Raritan, New Jersey, where they raised a family and Elizabeth led a traditional nineteenth-century woman's life. Any stories of her Civil War military service were kept closely held family secrets. Elizabeth never applied for a veteran's pension, although her husband did and received one. Following Martin's death in 1889, Elizabeth applied for benefits as his widow, not mentioning any service of her own during the war. A different aspect of her life was revealed in the application, however, when she described her relationship with Martin as "cohabitation without ceremony." Fortunately, the pension bureau accepted the common-law status of her marriage and approved her monthly stipend.

Following Elizabeth Niles' death on September 13, 1920, at age 76, her grown sons announced her military service in her obituary, and the account was picked up by a Washington, DC paper, which scrambled the story, listing her age as 92 and her unit as the 4th New Jersey Infantry, probably because she was a New Jersey resident. These errors have persisted in print to the present day. While there is no decisive provenance to Elizabeth Niles' saga, her service as a soldier has been widely accepted. She is buried in Somerville's New Somerville Cemetery, most likely in the unmarked grave next to her husband. (Blanton & Cook, *They Fought Like Demons*; Niles Pension File)

Robert Silverman
Diana Newman

Charles Smith Olden was born in Stony Brook, near Princeton, on February 19, 1799, to an old and established New Jersey Quaker family. He graduated from Lawrenceville School and worked as a clerk in several businesses in New Jersey and New Orleans before inheriting his uncle's estate, after which he became a "gentleman farmer," a director of the Trenton Banking Company, and a politician.

Olden served several terms in the New Jersey state senate as a Whig. When that party went defunct, he joined New Jersey's "Opposition Party," an alliance of former Whigs, "Know Nothing" nativists and Republicans, and was that party's successful candidate for governor in 1859. The "Opposition Party" evolved into the "Union Party" and finally the Republican Party. As the secession crisis loomed, Olden became known as a moderate, initially opposing the extension of slavery in the territories, yet willing to allow it to exist in the South. He was a proponent of the Washington Peace Conference of February 1861, and even attended, the only governor to do so. Although Olden was reportedly prepared to forego his opposition to the extension of slavery in return for peace, after the Confederates fired on Fort Sumter he strongly supported the Union war effort by energetically raising both money and troops. Historian William Gillette considers Olden "one of the North's great war governors."

Charles Smith Olden
(John W. Kuhl)

The New Jersey Constitution of 1844 prohibited Olden from running again for governor, and at the end of his three-year term he was succeeded by Democrat **Joel Parker** in 1863. After the war, he served as a judge on the New Jersey Court of Errors and Appeals (Supreme Court) from 1868 to 1873. He also served as treasurer of the College of New Jersey, now Princeton University, from 1845 to 1869, and as a state riparian commissioner. Olden died on April 7, 1876, and is buried at the Stony Brook Meeting House Cemetery in Princeton. Drumthwacket, his former home in Princeton, now much expanded, is currently the New Jersey governor's official residence. (http://www.drumthwacket.org/; Lurie & Mappen, *Encyclopedia of New Jersey*; Gillette, *Jersey Blue*; Stellhorn & Birkner, *The Governors of New Jersey*)

Dr. David G. Martin

Cortlandt Parker was born on June 27, 1818, in Perth Amboy into a family that had settled in America in the 17th century. He graduated from Rutgers College at the age of eighteen, first in a class that included a future associate justice of the New Jersey Supreme Court, a U.S. senator and secretary of state, and a governor of New Jersey. He moved to Newark, where he became a lawyer especially noted for his abilities as a litigator.

Originally a Whig, Parker opposed the slave trade and the extension of slavery into the territories. After the death of the Whig Party, he became one of the original founders of the Republican Party in New Jersey. Parker was a tireless campaigner for the presidential candidacies of both John Fremont and Abraham Lincoln, even though in the latter

Cortlandt Parker (The Parker Family)

case he had initially backed William Seward for the nomination. After the war began, Parker supported the Union cause to the point that his life and his home were threatened during the Newark draft disturbances of 1863. Among other military appointments, he helped **George W. Mindil** obtain a commission as colonel and the command of the 27th New Jersey Infantry, which later gained Mindil a similar position with the 33rd New Jersey.

With the end of the war, Parker worked on behalf of former slaves. When the New Jersey state legislature rejected the Fourteenth Amendment, his efforts kept the amendment on the legislative calendar until it finally passed. Parker declined offers of numerous state and federal offices, including minister to both Russia and the Austro-Hungarian Empire, and a position on the New Jersey Court of Errors and Appeals (Supreme Court). He died in Newark on July 29, 1907, at the age of 89. (Colie, "Cortlandt Parker")

John Zinn.

Joel Parker was born in Freehold on November 24, 1816. A Princeton graduate, Parker studied law under the tutelage of the state's chief justice, was admitted to the bar in 1842, practiced law in Freehold and became involved in Democratic Party politics. He defeated Newark mayor and prominent copperhead Moses Bigelow for the Democratic gubernatorial nomination in 1862 and went on to score a landslide victory over Republican **Marcus L. Ward**.

Parker served as governor from 1863 through 1866, and earned a solid reputation as one of the best war governors in the nation. He was an honest, patriotic and efficient administrator as well as being politically adept. Parker strongly criticized the Lincoln administration, vigorously questioning the constitutionality of several of the president's wartime measures, including the suspension of habeas corpus and the Emancipation Proclamation, and considered peace efforts with the Confederacy worth exploring. Those disagreements aside, Governor Parker was a "War Democrat" who actively supported the Union cause, did his utmost to meet troop-recruitment quotas and did not tolerate New Jerseyans who would undermine the federal war effort.

Joel Parker (John W. Kuhl)

Joel Parker grave marker in Maplewood Cemetery, Freehold. (Henry F. Ballone)

A "favorite son" presidential candidate at the 1868 Democratic National Convention, Parker was re-elected governor in 1870. The first New Jersey governor ever elected more than once by the direct vote of the people, he championed public education, fought bribery in the awarding of state offices, reformed the court system and helped break railroad monopolies. He later served in other state offices, including attorney general and as a judge on the state Court of Errors and Appeals (Supreme Court). He was nominated once more for governor in the 1880s, but declined. Parker died on January 2, 1888, and was buried at Maplewood Cemetery, Freehold. He is remembered as one of New Jersey's greatest nineteenth-century public officials. (Gillette, *Jersey Blue*; Lurie & Mappen, *Encyclopedia of New Jersey*; Stellhorn & Birkner, *The Governors of New Jersey*)

Edward S. Hoch

William Henry Parsons (William D. Parsons)

William Henry Parsons was born on April 23, 1826, near Elizabeth, New Jersey. His family subsequently moved to Montgomery, Alabama, where his father ran a shoe factory. Parsons joined the 2nd United States Dragoons during the war with Mexico, and following the war settled first in Tyler, Texas, and then in Waco. He published newspapers in Tyler and Waco, became a lawyer and was very involved in Democratic Party politics.

During the first year of the Civil War, "Wild Bill" Parsons was commissioned colonel of the 12th Texas Cavalry. By the autumn of 1862, he succeeded to brigade command and earned several citations in campaigns in the Red River country. It was said of Parsons that "no commander west of the Mississippi could deliver more fiery, colorful, and enthusiastic speeches from the saddle."

With the end of the war, Parsons left the country for British Honduras, intending to settle there in the wake of Confederate defeat. He soon returned to Texas, however, where he adjusted to the new political order and cooperated with the postwar government, earning himself the pejorative title of a "scalawag" and the enmity of his former Rebel neighbors. Parsons served as a Republican in the Texas state senate and was appointed by President U. S. Grant as a Texas representative to the United States Centennial Committee in 1876.

In the later years of the nineteenth century, Parsons moved north once more, where he worked as an attorney and real estate broker in Baltimore and New York. Along with his younger brother Albert, a member of the Chicago Knights of Labor, he became a supporter of the growing American labor movement. Albert was arrested as a principal in the 1886 Haymarket Riot and, despite William's assistance in his defense at the trial, was convicted of murder and hanged. William Parsons, who was involved with all the major events of his nineteenth-century life, died in Chicago on October 2, 1907, and was buried in Mount Hope Cemetery in Hastings-on-Hudson, New York. (Allerdice, *More Generals in Gray*)

John W. Kuhl

George Washington Patterson was
born in 1830 in Howell, New Jersey, the son of
John C. and Sarah Patterson. Patterson married
Mary Ann Shepard on March 4, 1854, and in
1861 was a Freehold furniture dealer. He was
active in local politics as well, serving as a
member of the Monmouth County Board of
Chosen Freeholders. In the summer of 1862,
Patterson recruited men for the 14th New Jersey
Infantry and was appointed a first lieutenant in
Company G. In March 1864, he resigned his
commission due to disability.

George Washington Patterson
(New Jersey State Archives)

Back in Monmouth County, Patterson ran a store
in Adelphia with his brother and then worked as
a horse and cattle dealer. He returned to politics
as well, and was appointed inspector of the New
Jersey state prison in 1871, served as tax collector
of Freehold Township from 1871 to 1874, and was a state assemblyman from 1873
to 1875. Patterson's political career appeared to come to an abrupt end with his
1875 conviction for embezzling $13,000 in tax revenues from Freehold, which
earned him a five-month sentence in the county jail. He was resilient, however,
and after his release moved to Asbury Park, where he worked as a butcher and
volunteer fireman, and became an influential Democratic Party leader, although
he did fail in two attempts to gain election as a state senator.

Using his considerable political connections, in 1888 Patterson prevailed upon
United States Senator and New York and Long Branch Railroad President Rufus
Blodgett to give his son Joe a job as freight agent in Asbury Park. Asbury was a
prohibition town, and when the raucous Joe turned the freight depot into a saloon
from which he and his tipsy friends sallied forth to the boardwalk and beach in
pursuit of women, they ran afoul of strict moralist and Asbury founder James A
Bradley. Physical threats and profane insults led to a court case in which the elder
Patterson had to be restrained from assaulting Bradley in a "frenzy of excitement
and passion."

George W. Patterson died of pneumonia on January 9, 1890, and more than 1,500
people attended the funeral of "one of the best known Democratic politicians in the
state." He is buried in Mount Prospect Cemetery in Neptune. (Bilby & Ziegler,
Asbury Park; Saretzky & Osovitz, *The Civil War and Monmouth County*)

Joseph G. Bilby

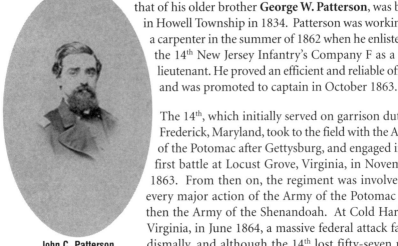

John C. Patterson, whose career differed considerably from that of his older brother **George W. Patterson**, was born in Howell Township in 1834. Patterson was working as a carpenter in the summer of 1862 when he enlisted in the 14th New Jersey Infantry's Company F as a first lieutenant. He proved an efficient and reliable officer and was promoted to captain in October 1863.

The 14th, which initially served on garrison duty at Frederick, Maryland, took to the field with the Army of the Potomac after Gettysburg, and engaged in its first battle at Locust Grove, Virginia, in November 1863. From then on, the regiment was involved in every major action of the Army of the Potomac and then the Army of the Shenandoah. At Cold Harbor, Virginia, in June 1864, a massive federal attack failed dismally, and although the 14th lost fifty-seven men killed, Captain Patterson, leading a fourteen-man detail, penetrated the enemy defensive line, outflanked a Rebel regiment and captured over 100 prisoners. In October 1864, at Cedar Creek, Virginia, he personally led several charges that saved an artillery battery from capture. Patterson's superb combat leadership was recognized by his promotion to major in January 1865, and his subsequent brevet promotions to lieutenant colonel and colonel in March 1865.

John C. Patterson
(New Jersey State Archives)

Patterson was mustered out of the service with his regiment in June 1865. In the postwar years, he worked for the United States Life Saving Service at Sandy Hook and Avon, and was credited with saving 147 persons from drowning. He became police chief, justice of the peace and building inspector of Ocean Grove in 1871, and also served as president of the Monmouth County Board of Elections. Patterson died on May 14, 1918, and was buried at the Ardena Baptist Church Cemetery in Adelphia. (Bilby & Goble, *Remember You Are Jerseymen*; Saretzky & Osovitz, *The Civil War and Monmouth County*)

A portrayal of one of the few Union successes at Cold Harbor, where Patterson captured more than 100 Confederates. (*Harper's Weekly*)

Joseph G. Bilby

James Olden Paxson was born in 1835 in Trenton, New Jersey, the son of former state treasurer Stacy Paxson. On June 24, 1861, he enlisted in the 48th New York Volunteers, a unit that recruited men in New Jersey, Connecticut and Massachusetts, earning the regiment the nickname the "Continental Guard." The 48th was also known as "Perry's Saints," after Colonel James H. Perry, its first commander, who had once attended West Point, but in 1861 was a prominent New York Methodist minister.

James Olden Paxson
(New Jersey State Archives)

Paxson was commissioned a first lieutenant in the 48th's Company D. The company's recruits, who nicknamed themselves the "Die No Mores," were all New Jerseyans, mostly from Monmouth and Mercer Counties. After preliminary training at Fort Hamilton in Brooklyn, in September the 48th left for Washington, and moved from there to Port Royal, South Carolina, where the regiment first saw action assaulting two Confederate fortifications. In April 1862, the 48th fought at the siege of Fort Pulaski, Georgia, and in June 1863, with Paxson now a captain commanding Company D, landed on Hilton Head Island, South Carolina, then moved on to the siege of Charleston. The regiment was assigned to the same brigade as the 54th Massachusetts Infantry and attacked Battery Wagner on July 18, 1863, alongside that famed African-American regiment. In the course of that disastrous assault, which cost the 48th almost 250 casualties, Captain Paxson was severely wounded by artillery fire. One account notes that "he [Paxson] was among the first to fall in crossing the ditch of the fort. Both legs were shattered at the knees." Paxson was evacuated with other wounded to Beaufort, South Carolina, "lying on a mattress on the floor of the steamboat Mary Benton." In frequent episodes of delirium he cried out "'Come on die-no-mores. Come on boys', the words he used as the regiment took the double quick and plunged into the seething abyss of death and destruction."

During the course of the Civil War, the 48th lost eighteen of its officers, sixteen of them at Battery Wagner, the most of any regiment, even the 54th, in that fight. Captain James Olden Paxson died of his wounds on July 31, 1863. His body was returned to New Jersey and buried at Mercer Cemetery in Trenton. (Nichols & Scaife, *Perry's Saints*)

Thomas R. Burke Jr.

Charles A. Pettit was born in New York in 1846 and was living in Newark when, on August 17, 1863, he joined Company F of the 33rd New Jersey Infantry as a musician. Pettit's 43-year-old father, Sydney S. Pettit, mustered out after nine-months service with the 27th New Jersey Infantry on July 2, 1863, reenlisted in Company F as a private on the same day.

Although family tradition relayed in Pettit's obituary held that his father did not know his son had joined the army, this seems unlikely. The story that one or both Pettits were at Gettysburg, also related in the obituary, is clearly impossible, since the 27th was actually in Newark being mustered out of service during the battle of Gettysburg and the Pettits did not join the 33rd until more than a month after the

Charles A. Pettit (The Connelly Family)

battle. Such errors are not unusual in twentieth-century obituaries of Civil War veterans, however, as memories dimmed and journalists proved less than assiduous.

The Pettits, a New Jersey father-and-son soldier team, may have missed Gettysburg, but they had adventure enough in their time in service. The 33rd began its combat career at Chattanooga, fought under General Sherman in the Atlanta Campaign, after which it shed its colorful but now tattered Zouave uniforms, then marched with Sherman to the sea and up through the Carolinas. In January 1865, Sydney Pettit was promoted to corporal. The regiment was mustered out of service on July 17, 1865, in Washington, DC.

After the war, Sydney returned to work as a blacksmith in Newark. Charles, after a stint as a factory worker, became a professional clown and blackface minstrel as a member of the team of Pettit and White, and reportedly "traveled with nearly every circus in the country." When his entertainment career ended, Charles took a job in a Newark varnish company, perhaps the one owned by Civil War veteran **Franklin Murphy**. Sydney Pettit died on April 7, 1896, and Charles followed him on October 5, 1913. Both soldiers were buried in Pine Brook Cemetery in Morris County. (Pettit obituary clipping; Zinn, *The Mutinous Regiment*)

Joseph G. Bilby

Victor Piard was born in 1825 in Le Havre, France, and immigrated with his family to Philadelphia as a child. In 1842, Piard moved to Washington, DC, where he became a photographer for Anthony, Edwards & Company. While working in the capital, Piard took Daguerreotype images of members of Congress, which were later used as references to compose a woodcut engraving of the United States Senate chamber commemorating Henry Clay's 1842 farewell speech.

Piard married Joanne Barron of Woodbridge, New Jersey, in 1849, and then moved to Brooklyn where, in a less credential-conscious age, he practiced dentistry and the couple had two sons.

Victor Piard (James M. Madden)

In the early 1850s, he opened a photographic studio in New York City in partnership with Alexander Beckers. After the partners broke up, Piard ran a grocery store, then became a photographer for C.D. Fredericks.

In 1860, Piard opened his own studio in Jersey City. Photographic technology had improved to the point where *carte de visite* paper prints could be produced cheaply. During the Civil War, these photographs became immensely popular with soldiers as well as their families, who could now conveniently carry an inexpensive image of a loved one. Piard's studio "backmark" is commonly seen on *cartes de visite* of Hudson County soldiers.

Although prosperous, Piard became increasingly eccentric. In 1863, he rolled out a cannon of some sort and pointed it at city hall, perhaps to make an undisclosed political point. The stunt apparently did not create the result Piard hoped for, so he repeated it the following day, to no avail. Although Piard's newfound wealth enabled him to compete as a yachtsman in Hudson River regattas, there was a darker side to his prosperity. The "well known and wealthy resident of Jersey City" was, according to a *New York Times* report of September 28, 1876, found lying in a New York City gutter, intoxicated and robbed of his watch and money.

Competition caused Piard's business to slump in the 1870s and, remarried to a Jersey City woman after the death of his first wife, he moved to Oceanport, where he became a carpenter and boat builder. In failing health and paralyzed, Victor Piard died on February 11, 1901, in Oceanport. He is buried with his first wife in Trinity churchyard in Woodbridge. (*American Standard*; *New York Times*; *Red Bank Register*; Welling, *Photography in the Americas*)

James M. Madden

Edward Augustus Pierson was born in 1836 to a wealthy and socially prominent Newark family. A direct descendant of the Reverend Abraham Pierson, one of the Puritan founders of the city, Edward led a privileged life. He studied at the Newark Wesleyan Institute, graduated from the College of Physicians and Surgeons in 1858 and opened an office practice shortly after graduation. When the Civil War began, Pierson was commissioned as surgeon's mate of the 1st New Jersey Militia.

Edward Augustus Pierson
(New Jersey Historical Society)

Pierson's letters and diaries, in the collections of the New Jersey Historical Society, indicate that he did not enjoy army life. He was thoroughly miffed that **John Craven**, the regiment's surgeon, held higher rank than he. Pierson did not like camping out and spent many nights at the famed Willard Hotel in Washington rather than sleeping under canvas with his regiment. He confided that he got the "blues….so bad that if I had the money I should have thrown up my commission and started for home. I never was cut out for an army soldier or anything else." The young doctor sorely missed his creature comforts and the society of ladies. By late June, however, things improved as he came to know the "crème" of Washington society, was enjoying good food in the officer's mess and finally received his delayed pay.

Returning home after the regiment was mustered out in July, Pierson began to buy new furniture for his office. Perhaps under peer pressure to reenlist, he visited his colleague, Doctor Craven, daily to discuss his ambivalence about returning to the service. On the day that Craven returned to the army, Pierson wrote the commander of the Brooklyn Naval Hospital regarding a commission in the navy, and received a positive response. He was subsequently assigned to the frigate *St. Lawrence* and was on board that ship during a memorable contest with the *Merrimac* in 1862, narrowly escaping death or injury when a shell smashed into his room and struck within a few feet of his head. While subsequently stationed in Key West, Pierson contracted yellow fever and was sent north to recuperate. On recovery, he was assigned to the *Penobscot*, on blockade duty off Wilmington, North Carolina. While Pierson was serving on the *Penobscot* in 1863, a shell fired from a Confederate fort on shore crashed into his quarters, mortally wounding him. He died two hours later. Buried in Newark, he was remembered as a "young man of rare personal beauty, of vivacious manners, of remarkable memory, of great good nature, and a consistent Christian." (http://www.civilwarsurgeonsmemorial.org/; Pierson papers)

Valerie M. Josephson

Rodman McCamley Price was born on May 5, 1816, in Newton, Sussex County, attended Lawrenceville Academy and Princeton University, and then studied law. In 1840, he became a navy purser, a position dealing with payroll and supply. The Mexican War found him in California, appointed *alcalde* of Monterey by Commodore John D. Sloat. Price subsequently became Pacific Fleet purser with headquarters in San Francisco, engaging in land speculation and other businesses as a sideline to his official duties. A delegate to the California constitutional convention, he also ran unsuccessfully for Congress. Accused of misappropriating funds, Price was ordered east, but the charges were indefinitely postponed when the steamer carrying his records burned.

Rodman McCamley Price
(New Jersey State Archives)

Out of the navy in 1850, Price moved to Hoboken and began speculating on Wall Street as well as in California real estate. Elected to Congress in New Jersey's Fifth District as a Democrat, in 1853 he successfully ran for governor, with "fiery apple brandy flowing freely at rallies." Governor Price reformed New Jersey's school system, founded the first normal school or teacher's college, worked with New York on harbor facilities, and expanded the judicial system and the state insane asylum.

On the national level, Price was far less progressive. He supported allowing slavery in the territories and other Southern positions. To Price, slavery was "no sin" but a normal way of conducting race relations. He campaigned for Stephen A. Douglas in the election of 1860 and in February 1861 was a delegate to the "Peace Conference" convened in Washington in an attempt to head off the Civil War. Once war broke out, however, he advocated that New Jersey secede and join the Confederacy, effectively ending his political career. When abolition became a war aim in 1863, Price ranted that Lincoln was "a traitor," who "stands reeking in the blood of his countrymen." Ironically, Price's son Francis, commissioned a first lieutenant in the 7th New Jersey Infantry, eventually rose to the rank of brevet brigadier general in the Union army.

In the postwar era, Rodman Price engaged in numerous failing business activities. In the early 1890s, revived inquiries into his alleged financial malfeasance in California resulted in his imprisonment. He was released due to ill health, and died on June 7, 1894, in Oakland. He was buried in nearby Mahwah. (Gillette, *Jersey Blue;* Lurie & Mappen, *Encyclopedia of New Jersey;* Lurie, *A New Jersey Anthology;* Stellhorn & Birkner, *The Governors of New Jersey*)

Joseph G. Bilby

William H. Reid was born a free African-American in Summerton, Virginia, on February 28, 1840. During the Civil War, he was conscripted by the Confederate government to build fortifications near New Bern, North Carolina. After federal troops captured New Bern in March 1862, Reid left Confederate service and the South, becoming a sailor on coastal vessels. Following this trade, he ended up in New York City in February 1864, where he enlisted in the 26th United States Colored Infantry. As a soldier in the 26th, Reid served as part of the garrison of Beaufort, South Carolina, from April though November of 1864 and participated in several raids along the coast. The 26th fought at Honey Hill and Devaux's Neck, South Carolina, in

William H. Reid grave marker (Rodney Snell, findagrave.com)

November and December 1864, and then returned to Beaufort. The regiment was mustered out of service in New York on August 28, 1865.

After his discharge, Reid settled in Red Bank, New Jersey, where he married a local girl named Hannah Van Breekle and bought a house on Mechanic Street. The couple had twelve children. Reid, described as "faithful, industrious and frugal" by his neighbors, worked as a caretaker, landscaper and handyman in Red Bank for the next fifty years. He was active in veterans' affairs as a member and then commander of the General **William Birney** Post of the GAR. Although Mrs. Reid died in 1897, her husband's health remained excellent well into the twentieth century. The former foot soldier made a practice of taking long walks every year on his birthday. His last trek took place in 1922, when the 82-year-old veteran marched from Red Bank to Freehold and back.

Prepared for every eventuality, Reid made his own coffin and dug his own grave in White Ridge Cemetery in Eatontown and lined it with brick, because he "did not want to bother or make trouble" for his children after his death. He didn't. One of the last survivors of his regiment, William H. Reid died in January of 1927. He was buried in White Ridge. (Bilby, *Forgotten Warriors*)

Joseph G. Bilby

Restless was sired by Rysdyk's Hambletonian, whose name headlines the famous annual race, in 1856 on the farm of William Rysdyk in Chester, New York. When he was six, Restless was given as a gift to Colonel Samuel Fowler of the 15th New Jersey Infantry as the colonel was about to leave for the field with his regiment. Raised in the late summer of 1862, the 15th was initially deployed in the defenses of Washington and then joined the Army of the Potomac after Antietam. Colonel

Rysdyk's Hambletonian, sire of Restless, circa 1870 in a Currier and Ives print.

Fowler never led the 15th into action, as an October bout with typhoid fever left him so debilitated he had to resign from the army. Restless continued in service, however, as the mount of the 15th's Chaplain **Alanson Haines**. Haines, known for his concern for the welfare of the regiment's men, believers or not, was one of New Jersey's finest Civil War military clergymen.

Chaplain Haines loaned Restless out to fellow officers on occasion, including, at one time or another, General A. T. A. Torbert, commander of the First New Jersey Brigade, as well as officers serving on the staffs of General John Sedgwick and General Philip Sheridan. The horse participated in all of the 15th's battles and bore the scars of several wounds received in action.

At the end of the war, Chaplain Haines brought Restless back to the family farm near Ogdensburg, New Jersey, where the horse spent the rest of his life in dignified retirement, as well cared for as his sire, who was sold to Jonas Seeley and became perhaps the most famous American horse of the nineteenth century. Restless, with less fame but as much respect as his father, "succumbed to the infirmities of age" at the age of thirty-three in November 1889, and was buried with military honors, his body wrapped in an American flag, in a conspicuous place on the Haines property. Unfortunately his gravesite has since been lost to the ages. (*NY Times* Obituary; Miller, "Recollections")

Robert F. MacAvoy

Joseph Warren Revere was born in Boston on May 18, 1812, a grandson of the famed patriot Paul Revere. Revere enlisted in the U.S. Navy in 1828, participated in the Seminole and Mexican Wars and eventually rose to the rank of lieutenant. He was cited for bravery in pulling down the California Republic "Bear Flag" and then raising the American flag over Sonoma, California. Revere resigned from the navy in 1850 and joined the Mexican army as a lieutenant colonel, serving through 1852, when he moved to Morristown, New Jersey. In 1854, he built a Greek Revival mansion on his 200 acre farm, "The Willows," west of town. He married Rosanna Duncan and the couple had five children.

Joseph Warren Revere (USAMHI/MOLLUS)

At the outbreak of the Civil War, Revere, unsuccessful in his attempt to rejoin the navy, gained a commission as colonel of the 7th New Jersey Infantry. He fought with that regiment in the Peninsula Campaign and at Second Bull Run, where he was cited for bravery in action. In October of 1862, Revere was promoted to brigadier general and assigned to command the "Excelsior Brigade," a New York unit with a large number of New Jerseyans in its ranks. During the battle of Chancellorsville, his division commander, General Hiram C. Berry, was killed and Revere assumed command of the division. After surveying the situation, Revere decided that the best course of action was to withdraw the division to the rear to reorganize, an act that left a hole in the Union line and led to his court martial for acting without orders. Revere was dismissed from the army but because of previous conduct later restored to his rank by President Lincoln and allowed to resign. In 1866, he was awarded the brevet rank of major general by act of Congress.

After the war, Revere traveled and wrote two memoirs, *Keel and Saddle* and *A Tour of Duty in California, Including a Description of the Gold Region*. He suffered declining health in the late 1870s and died in a Hoboken hotel on April 20, 1880. He was buried at Holy Rood Catholic Cemetery in Morristown. General Revere's former home has been renovated and is currently operated by the Morris County Parks Commission as "Fosterfields." (http://www.morrisparks.net/aspparks/ffmain.asp; Lurie & Mappen, *Encyclopedia of New Jersey*; Revere, *Keel and Saddle*)

Thomas R. Burke, Jr.

Fanny Lawrence Ricketts was born on May 8, 1834, into a wealthy Elizabeth, New Jersey, family, the daughter of an English businessman who owned estates in Jamaica. Her mother was the daughter of Captain Ricketts, an English army officer, and also a descendant of the famous Livingston family of New Jersey. In 1856, Fanny married Captain James Brewerton Ricketts, a professional army officer and distant cousin on her mother's side. Fanny's devotion to her husband was repeatedly displayed throughout the Civil War.

James & Fanny Lawrence Ricketts
(National Park Service)

On July 23, 1861, Fanny Ricketts learned that her husband had been severely wounded and captured two days earlier while commanding an artillery battery at the battle of Bull Run. She immediately set out in a borrowed light carriage and found him in a Confederate field hospital where she nursed his wounds and refused to leave his side, even after he was transferred to a makeshift Richmond hospital and, finally, Libby Prison. Fanny's continuous care was credited with saving her husband's leg and life. When Captain Ricketts was freed in a prisoner exchange six months later, Mrs. Ricketts traveled with him to Fairfax, Virginia, where he completed his recovery and Fanny regained her own damaged health.

Fanny Ricketts came to her husband's aid again during the war, nursing then Brigadier General Ricketts back to health after the September 1862 battle of Antietam, where his horse fell on his previously wounded leg. When General Ricketts, serving as Sixth Corps commander, suffered what was thought to be a mortal chest wound at the battle of Cedar Creek in October 1864, his wife, this time with a cavalry escort, rushed to his side. She was credited with helping to save his life yet again with her careful postoperative care, nursing him for four months after his surgery.

After the war, Fanny Ricketts resided with her husband and children in Washington, DC, where she outlived James by thirteen years and died on September 13, 1900. She was buried in Arlington National Cemetery beside her husband. Her son, Basil Norris Ricketts, who served in Teddy Roosevelt's Rough Riders during the Spanish-American War, is buried nearby. (Brockett & Vaughn, *Women's Work*; Larson, *White Roses*)

Robert Silverman
Diana Newman

William Boyd Robertson was born on June 21, 1821, in Scotland and immigrated to Salem, New Jersey, in the early 1840s, where he married his wife Caroline, who bore their six children. Robertson, a pharmacist by trade, raised Company A of the 24th New Jersey Infantry, a regiment recruited in Camden, Gloucester and Salem Counties in September 1862 for nine-months service, and was subsequently elected colonel by the regiment's other officers. The men of the 24th, armed with Belgian-made Vincennes rifles, left Camp Cadwallader in Beverly on September 30 by steamship for Philadelphia, where they boarded trains for Washington.

William Boyd Robertson (John W. Kuhl)

Although recruits for nine-months regiments were assured by New Jersey newspaper editors that they would not be thrown into the cauldron of combat, this proved not to be the case with the 24th. Robertson's regiment was assigned to the First Brigade of the Army of the Potomac's Second Corps' Third Division in early December. On December 13, at Fredericksburg, Virginia, he was ordered to lead the 24th in the Second Corps' assault on Marye's Heights. General Nathan Kimball addressed the regiment before the attack, asking the men to do their duty and to "remember you are Jerseymen." In the ensuing disaster, the 24th was shattered, losing 160 soldiers killed, wounded and missing. The regiment fought again at Chancellorsville in May 1863, suffering thirty-six more causalities.

The 24th New Jersey was mustered out of federal service on June 29, 1863, at Beverly, and Colonel Robertson returned to Salem, where he opened a china shop. By 1880, he had moved to Camden, was employed by the Pennsylvania Railroad and was a member of the William B. Hatch GAR Post. In 1888, he was living at the Presbyterian Mission at 840 Federal Street and working as a salesman. Colonel Robertson died on August 10, 1889, and was buried at the Old Camden Cemetery. His gray marble obelisk is one of the tallest undamaged grave markers still standing in that graveyard. The impressive monument is adorned with several trefoils, representing the badge of the Second Corps. An inscription indicates it was erected by "His Comrades of The Regiment," a testament to the enduring affections of the men he led up Marye's Heights and his now forgotten contribution to New Jersey's history. (http://www.dvrbs.com/people/camdenpeople-ColWilliamBRobertson.htm; Bilby & Goble, *Remember You Are Jerseymen*)

Thomas R. Burke Jr.

Washington Augustus Roebling
(New Jersey State Archives)

Washington Augustus Roebling was born on May 26, 1837, in Saxonburg, Pennsylvania, and moved to Trenton with his family in 1848. Roebling graduated from Rensselaer Polytechnic Institute as a civil engineer in 1857 and then began working for his father, John Roebling, in the family wire-rope manufacturing and bridge-building business. He enlisted as a private in Trenton's "A Company, New Jersey National Guard Infantry" on April 16, 1861. The company never left New Jersey, and after two months of guard duty at the state arsenal, Roebling was discharged and enlisted in the 6th New York Independent Battery, Light Artillery, a unit raised in Rahway. Promoted to sergeant after four months, he was commissioned a lieutenant in February of 1862.

Roebling was assigned to staff duty, where his engineering expertise was of great value, and served in that capacity for the rest of his time in the army. While on duty in an observation balloon, he filed the initial report of the Army of Northern Virginia's June 1863 move north. As an aide to General Gouverneur K. Warren at Gettysburg, Roebling was one of the first officers to reach the critical Little Round Top terrain and assist in preparing that position to resist Confederate attack. Roebling resigned his commission in January 1865, having attained the rank of brevet colonel.

Following his military service, Washington Roebling returned to the Roebling business interests in Trenton and played a major role in the building of the Brooklyn Bridge, one of the most significant engineering and construction achievements of the nineteenth century. When John Roebling died suddenly and tragically from tetanus, Washington took over the company and the project. His own health was subsequently severely impaired through a combination of "caisson disease" or "the bends," anxiety and overwork. Even though ill, however, Roebling continued to play an important role in the successful completion of the bridge, with the vital assistance of his wife, Emily Warren Roebling, General Warren's sister, whom he had met during the war. Other than periods in Brooklyn and Troy, New York, Roebling and his family lived in Trenton, where he managed the family business, John A. Roebling's Sons. Washington A. Roebling died at his home in Trenton on July 21, 1926. He was buried at Cold Spring Cemetery in Cold Spring, New York, next to his wife. (Lurie & Mappen, *Encyclopedia of New Jersey*; McCullough, *The Great Bridge; NY Times* Obituary)

John Zinn

Julius David Rosé was born in Hanover, Germany, in 1824. His father, a Lutheran minister, saw to it that Julius had an excellent education, and he ultimately received two doctoral degrees, in medicine and languages, as well as becoming an ordained Lutheran minister. Rosé immigrated to the U.S. in 1845 and married Elizabeth Krieg in 1847. They had one child, a son named George. Rosé converted to Episcopalianism in 1848 and was ordained an Episcopal priest on August 12, 1849. He later founded St. Matthew's German Protestant Episcopal Church in Newark.

Julius David Rosé (Fr. David Moreno)

On August 23, 1861, Father Rosé volunteered to serve as chaplain of the newly formed 7th New Jersey Infantry, with the aim of providing soldiers with spiritual guidance and counseling. A chaplain's duties in the Civil War army varied widely, and included conducting weekly religious services, blessing the troops as they moved into battle or on special occasions, ministering to the needs of the wounded and dying, acting as an educator and even as regimental librarian or postmaster. Since Rosé was a medical doctor, he was uniquely qualified to assist in caring for the wounded at field hospitals. In the spring of 1863, General Joseph Hooker personally commended Rosé twice for his service.

Rosé's medical knowledge did not provide him with personal immunity. In early May of 1862, while on the march, he contracted malaria coupled with a severe case of diarrhea, a combination of afflictions that would plague him for the rest of his life. Following the battle of Gettysburg, Rosé fell victim to sunstroke, which, given his already weakened condition, hastened the end of his military career; he received a medical discharge on September 21, 1863.

After his discharge, Father Rosé returned to his rectorship in Newark, a post he resigned in 1869 to enter the field of education, another area for which he was uniquely prepared. He founded St. John's Hall in Summit, later became headmaster of St. Stephen's School in Millburn and in 1880 founded the Heights Academy on Old Short Hills Road in Short Hills. Even with his heavy workload, Rosé still found time to officiate at weddings and baptisms. He was also very active in veterans' affairs, and attended and spoke at many reunions. Julius David Rosé died at Christ Church, Short Hills, on September 12, 1890, and was buried at Saint Stephen's Episcopal Cemetery in Millburn. (Archives of the Episcopal Diocese of New Jersey)

Father David G. Moreno
Thomas R. Burke Jr.

Theodore Runyon (Library of Congress)

Theodore Runyon was born in Somerville, New Jersey, on October 25, 1822, and graduated from Yale University in 1842. Admitted to the New Jersey bar in 1846, Runyon moved to Newark to establish a law practice. In 1853, he became Newark City Attorney and three years later moved up to the position of Newark City Counselor, a job he held through 1864. Runyon was also very active in the New Jersey Militia and Governor **Charles Olden** assigned him to command the militia brigade the state sent to Washington at the beginning of the Civil War. Although the brigade participated in the First Bull Run Campaign as part of a division including the 1st, 2nd and 3rd New Jersey Infantry, all under Runyon's command, the Jerseyans saw no action. Runyon was mustered out with his brigade on July 31, 1861, and performed no active military service for the rest of the war. He was, however, promoted to brevet major general in the New Jersey Militia in February of 1862.

Back in Newark, Runyon resumed his law practice and continued to serve as city counselor. In July of 1863 he, along with Mayor Moses Bigelow, helped quiet an angry mob threatening the offices of the *Newark Daily Mercury*, the city's Republican newspaper, at the height of the New York City draft riots. As a leading Democrat, his call for calm carried a lot of

Theodore Runyon's brigade parades before President Lincoln in Washington in 1861. (John Bielamowicz)

credibility with the people of the city. Runyon was elected Mayor of Newark in 1864 and went on to run unsuccessfully for governor in 1865. He was subsequently appointed Chancellor of New Jersey, the head of the state's judiciary, a position he held for fourteen years. In 1893, Runyon was appointed ambassador to Germany by President Grover Cleveland. Although he had some history of health problems, it was apparently still something of a shock when he succumbed to heart disease in Berlin on January 27, 1896. Theodore Runyon was buried in Mount Pleasant Cemetery in Newark. (Bilby & Goble, *Remember You Are Jerseymen; Trenton Times* Obituary)

John Zinn

Nathan "Nate" Salsbury was born in Freeport, Illinois, in 1846. On February 24, 1865, he enlisted in the 156th Illinois Infantry for one year's service. On March 28, the 156th was ordered to Chattanooga, Tennessee. The regiment was transferred to Memphis in June and mustered out of service on September 20, 1865. The 156th performed garrison duty and did not engage in any battles, but had two men wounded, one accidentally. While on duty with the unit, Salsbury reputedly sang and danced to entertain his fellow soldiers. In later years, he spun for the press a wartime tale far removed from his actual rather mundane military history. According to Salsbury, he joined the 15th Illinois Infantry in 1861 as "the youngest soldier in the field." He claimed that he was wounded and discharged, yet reenlisted "in several different regiments" and fought everywhere from Chickamauga to Texas, and left the army with $20,000 in poker winnings. No evidence exists for any of these claims.

Nathan "Nate" Salsbury
(Library of Congress)

Although much of what Nate Salsbury said over the years can be taken with far more than the usual cautionary grain of salt, what is known is that after the war he was affiliated with several itinerant theater companies as an actor, writer and producer before organizing a company of his own known as the Troubadours. His growing success in the field led to an acquaintance with "Buffalo Bill" Cody, and in 1883 he became Cody's business partner in the famous Wild West Show, which he managed for the rest of his life. Without Salsbury, there would have been no legendary "Wild West." His biggest business coup was signing Annie Oakley.

His fortune made, Salsbury and his wife, Rachel Samuels, settled in Long Branch, New Jersey, where he bought a house on Liberty Street and lived between tours and raised his four children. He was active in civic affairs, served as president of the Long Branch Property Holders Organization, and was also involved in local real estate development. Salsbury's $200,000 luxury oceanfront cottage development, known as "The Reservation," was razed in the 1980s, when the property became Seven Presidents County Park. Nate Salsbury died in Long Branch on December 24, 1902, from "stomach trouble." (Lurie & Mappen, *Encyclopedia of New Jersey*; *NY Times* Obituary)

Joseph G. Bilby

Alvin Satterthwaite was born in Philadelphia in 1838, but his family soon moved to a New Jersey farm. While still very young, Alvin left the farm to work at his uncle's newspaper office in Camden, New Jersey, where he was hired to pick up papers in Philadelphia, bring them to Camden and deliver them to subscribers. At the age of fifteen, Satterthwaite began working in a drug store and also attended high school, eventually entering the Philadelphia College of Medicine, from where he graduated in 1858. Shortly thereafter, Doctor Satterthwaite moved to Florida, where he practiced with a Doctor Overstreet at Columbus on the Suwannee River. When the political turmoil that led to the Civil War arose, he left the practice and headed home to New Jersey from where, after the war's outbreak, he applied to the navy for a surgeon's commission, but was apparently turned down because of his short stature.

Alvin Satterthwaite (John W. Kuhl)

The army had no problem with his height. Satterthwaite rode to Princeton and applied directly to Governor **Charles Olden** for a medical position with one of the New Jersey militia units. The first applicant, he was appointed assistant surgeon of the 4th New Jersey Militia. That three-month-service regiment returned home in July 1861, and Satterthwaite was commissioned assistant surgeon in the 7th New Jersey Infantry in August. On July 19, 1862, he was promoted to surgeon of the 12th New Jersey Infantry. William Haines, a private in the 12th and author of the 1897 *History of the Men of Co. F., with Description of the Marches and Battles of the 12th NJ Vols.*, had the greatest praise for Doctor Satterthwaite. According to Haines, Satterthwaite "was with the regiment from the time it left Woodbury till its muster out, with the exception of a short time that he served as brigade surgeon. He was a bold and skillful operator, though very conservative." Satterthwaite served with the 12th in all its battles through the end of the war, including Chancellorsville, Gettysburg, Bristoe Station, Mine Run, Morton's Ford, the Wilderness, Spotsylvania, Cold Harbor, Petersburg, Reams Station, Fort Hell and Hatchers Run.

After the war, Doctor Satterthwaite resettled at Mariners Harbor on Staten Island, New York, and continued the practice of medicine until 1872. He died on February 16, 1873 at the age of 35 and was buried at Mount Holly Cemetery. (http://www.civilwarsurgeonsmemorial.org/; Haines, *Men of Company F*; Longacre, *Gettysburg and Beyond*)

Valerie M. Josephson

Sauerbier mark on a sword blade.
(John W. Kuhl)

Henry Sauerbier was born in Prussia in 1822. Trained as a cutler and edged-tool maker, he immigrated to Newark, New Jersey, in 1848 and went into business with John H. Crawford. In 1855, Sauerbier opened Henry Sauerbier & Company in Newark, at that time the fastest growing industrial city in the country. He specialized in the manufacture of saddles and harness as well as leatherworking tools. Sometime between 1856 and 1860, Sauerbier added military swords to his product line.

By the late 1850s, Sauerbier's business was in trouble, as were many in the wake of the economic collapse following the fiscal "Panic" of 1857. The Civil War brought more financial gloom to Newark merchants and manufacturers like Sauerbier as the conflict cut off the city's lucrative Southern trade. Eventually, however, massive federal spending occasioned by the war returned prosperity to a city that produced military necessities in the form of clothing, leather goods and precision metalwork.

On August 15, 1861, Sauerbier received his first government contract for 100 infantry officer's swords, featuring brass-mounted iron scabbards. He also made Model 1840 "wrist breaker" cavalry sabers and non-regulation sabers and swords for private purchase. Sauerbier became well known for ornate silver and pewter-mounted presentation swords decorated with detailed etchings and precious stone inlays. Surviving specimens indicate that the Model 1850 foot officer and Model 1860 staff and field officer swords were his best sellers. Sauerbier also sold swords to other retailers, including Schuyler, Hartley & Graham of New York, and supplied blades to smaller sword makers. In 1864 he expanded his business interests into the financial sector, as a bank trustee of Newark's Dime Savings Institution.

With the end of the war, Sauerbier's main manufacturing effort returned to making hand tools, and he was granted several patents for innovative and improved designs in the postwar period. Around 1870, Sauerbier brought his sons Henry Jr. and Julius to the business, changing its name to H. Sauerbier & Sons. Sauerbier's date of death is unknown, and, although one source lists it as 1878, he was apparently still alive and living with his wife, Augusta Rose, and seven children in Newark in 1880. The Sauerbier family business itself ended in 1887. (Peterson, *American Sword*; Tuttle, *How Newark Became Newark*)

Thomas R. Burke Jr.

Henry Washington Sawyer was born on March 16, 1829, in Egypt, Pennsylvania. He moved to Cape May, New Jersey, in 1848, where he married Harriet Eldredge in 1850. The couple had three children, one of whom survived to adulthood. In April 1861, Sawyer, a firm Unionist, carried letters from Governor **Charles Olden** to Washington, then served a brief hitch in a Pennsylvania militia unit. Back in New Jersey in August, he enlisted as a second lieutenant in "Halsted's Horse," a cavalry regiment organized by Republican politician William Halsted.

**Henry Washington Sawyer
(New Jersey State Archives)**

Unfortunately, Colonel Halsted's political skills did not translate into military ones; the regiment was an administrative disaster, rife with nepotism, incompetence and internal feuding. In response, Governor Olden assigned Lieutenant Colonel **Joseph Kargé**, a Polish immigrant and veteran cavalryman, to reorganize it. Kargé's reforms, coupled with the resignations and dismissals of Halsted and his cronies, the appointment of **Percy Wyndham** as colonel and a new designation as the 1st New Jersey Cavalry, set the regiment on the road to becoming one of the best cavalry units in the Union army.

Sawyer proved a competent officer, and saw his share of action. Injured when his horse fell on his leg at Woodstock, Virginia, in June 1862, he was later shot in the stomach near Aldie in October, but survived. Promoted to captain, he was shot yet again in the thigh and neck, thrown from his horse and captured at Brandy Station in June 1863.

Sawyer's captivity brought national fame. When Confederate officers captured in Kentucky were hanged as spies, Sawyer and another prisoner were chosen by lot to be hanged in retaliation. Harriet Sawyer, a competent woman used to getting her way, personally visited President Lincoln with her congressman in tow, resulting in an implied Union counterthreat to hang General Lee's son, then a Union prisoner. Sawyer was eventually exchanged, promoted to major, and mustered out in July 1865.

Major Sawyer returned to Cape May, where he managed several hotels before opening his own, the Chalfonte, in the mid-1870s. After Harriet's death in 1889, he remarried and had two more children. Sawyer served on the local city council and was appointed to several offices, including superintendent of New Jersey's Life Saving Stations. He died of a heart attack at Cape May on October 16, 1893, and was buried in the Presbyterian Church Cemetery in Cold Spring. (http://www.bivouacbooks.com/bbv2i2s6.htm; Longacre, *Jersey Cavaliers*)

Joseph G. Bilby

Julian Scott was born in Johnson, Vermont, on February 15, 1846. Scott was a student at the Lamoille Academy when he enlisted at age 15 as a musician in the 3rd Vermont Infantry, a regiment of the famed Vermont Brigade, in 1861. He was awarded the Medal of Honor for saving fellow soldiers at the battle of Lee's Mills, Virginia, on April 16, 1862, during the siege of Yorktown. Scott's citation relates that he "crossed the creek under a terrific fire of musketry several times to assist in bringing off the wounded." Later that year, he was detailed to hospital service in New York.

Julian Scott (National Archives)

Scott, who had sketched the scenes of war around him during his enlistment, received a disability discharge in April 1863, and soon afterward enrolled in the National Academy of Design in New York to study art. He visited the army again in 1864, but this time as an artist. He also studied with noted artist Emanuel Leutze, best known for "Washington Crossing the Delaware," and in Europe at Paris and Stuttgart. In the postwar era, Scott became a noted American historical artist, best known for his Civil War paintings, including a work on the Vermont Brigade's stand at the battle of Cedar Creek in October of 1864 that he completed in 1874, which still hangs in the Vermont State House. Another Scott masterpiece is his rendering of the death of General John Sedgwick at the battle of Spotsylvania. Scott also traveled west in 1889 and painted Native-American scenes in Arizona and New Mexico.

In 1870, when he became an associate of the National Academy of Design, Julian Scott settled with his wife and family in Plainfield, New Jersey, where he opened a studio on West Front Street. Recruited by fellow Medal of Honor recipient **James Madison Drake** of Elizabeth, always on the lookout for good publicity, into the "Veteran Zouaves" marching and social club, he became the unit's honorary "colonel." Scott lived the rest of his life in Plainfield, where he died on July 4, 1901. He is buried in Hillside Cemetery in Scotch Plains. His painting of General Sedgwick's death is in the collection of the Plainfield Historical Society. (Lurie & Mappen, *Encyclopedia of New Jersey*; *NY Times* Obituary)

Joseph G. Bilby

William Joyce Sewell was born in Castlebar, County Mayo, Ireland, on December 6, 1835, and immigrated to the United States in 1851. Sewell moved from Chicago to Camden in 1860, where he raised a company for the 5th New Jersey Infantry and was commissioned a captain in August 1861. He was promoted to lieutenant colonel of the 5th in July 1862 and colonel of the regiment that November.

William Joyce Sewell (John W. Kuhl)

When General **Gershom Mott**, commanding the Second New Jersey Brigade, was wounded at Chancellorsville on May 3, 1863, Sewell took command of the brigade, which was beginning to fall back, rallied it and led it in a successful counterattack. He was badly wounded while leading his regiment on July 2 at Gettysburg, and although he returned to duty for the spring campaign of 1864, Colonel Sewell still suffered from the effects of his injury and resigned his commission in July. He recovered enough to be appointed colonel of the 38th New Jersey Infantry in November 1864, and ended the war in command of that regiment. A highly regarded officer, Sewell received brevet promotions to brigadier and major general in March 1865 for his gallantry and leadership at Chancellorsville and other wartime service.

In the postwar era, Sewell was appointed a brigadier general in the New Jersey National Guard and participated in the selection of the site for the Guard's Sea Girt camp in 1885. He also became vice president of the West Jersey Railroad and was a partner in a number of other business enterprises in the Camden area, including banks and real estate developments, as well as insurance, steamship, ferry and electric trolley companies. General Sewell was active in Republican Party politics and became the party's Camden boss and a major political figure in the state. He was elected and served as a New Jersey state senator from 1872 to 1880, and then as a U.S. senator in 1881 and again in 1895. In 1896, senator Sewell was awarded the Medal of Honor for his actions at Chancellorsville. He died in Camden on December 27, 1901, and is buried in Harleigh Cemetery in that city. (Bilby & Goble, *Remember You are Jerseymen*; Lurie & Mappen, *Encyclopedia of NJ*)

Joseph G. Bilby

Alexander Shaler was born in Haddam, Connecticut, on March 19, 1827, and moved with his family at an early age to New York City, where he joined the New York State Militia, rising to major in the city's elite 7th Regiment. While a captain in the 7th, he lived in Hoboken, New Jersey, and also served as Colonel of the 1st Regiment, Hudson Brigade of the New Jersey Militia. Military affairs were Shaler's passion, but he also owned a successful stonemasonry business. He married Mary McMurry in 1847 and the couple had five children.

Alexander Shaler (USAMHI/MOLLUS)

In June 1861, upon returning from Washington after thirty-days duty with the 7th, Shaler was commissioned lieutenant colonel of the 65th New York Infantry. He was subsequently promoted to colonel and brigadier general, and served as a brigade commander at Chancellorsville. In the winter of 1863-1864, Shaler commanded the Confederate prison on Johnson's Island, Ohio. Returning to the Army of the Potomac in the spring, he was captured along with his thoroughbred bay stallion in the battle of the Wilderness. Shaler's horse became the property of Confederate General John B. Gordon, and he gained a unique if dubious distinction as the only Union officer who had commanded a Union prison and then became an inmate of a Confederate prison. After his eventual exchange, Shaler was assigned to the Department of Arkansas. He was brevetted major general, mustered out of service on August 24, 1865, and subsequently awarded the Medal of Honor for gallantry during the battle of Chancellorsville.

After the war, Shaler became major general of the New York National Guard and held many New York City municipal positions. He was also active in numerous military, civic and social organizations, and credited as one of the founders of the National Rifle Association. His tenure as a National Guard Commander was a tumultuous one. A fellow officer accused him of incompetence and he was later charged with corruption in making his choices for armory sites. Although tried, Shaler was never convicted of any wrongdoing, but was forced to retire from the National Guard and his position on the New York City board of health.

After his retirement, Shaler returned to New Jersey, settled in Ridgefield and served as president of the board of education, commissioner of the board of health and then mayor (1899-1901). General Shaler died December 28, 1911, and is buried in the English Neighborhood Reformed Church Cemetery in Ridgefield. (Warner, *Generals in Blue*)

James M. Madden

George Henry Sharpe (USAMHI/MOLLUS)

George Henry Sharpe was born on February 26, 1828, in Kingston, New York, and graduated with honors from Rutgers College in New Brunswick, New Jersey. He subsequently attended Yale Law School, passed the bar in 1849 and in 1850 received an A.M. from Rutgers. Sharpe studied in Europe for several years while serving as a diplomat at the U.S. legations in Vienna and Rome. In 1855, he returned to the United States, married Caroline Hasbrouck, the daughter of the president of Rutgers, and practiced law.

At the outbreak of the Civil War, Sharpe served as captain of Company B of the 20th New York State Militia until the regiment's muster out in August 1861. The following August, he was commissioned colonel of the 120th New York Infantry. Sharpe led his regiment at Fredericksburg in December, was appointed a deputy provost marshal general in February 1863, and assigned to organize the newly created Bureau of Military Information. Intelligence historians commonly credit Sharpe with establishing the first modern intelligence-gathering organization. He served on the staffs of Generals Hooker and Meade, advising them on enemy activities. On the evening of July 2, 1863, Sharpe addressed Meade's council of war at Gettysburg, and his presentation on enemy capabilities and probable intentions was influential in the general's decision to hold his ground, resulting in the successful repulse of Pickett's Charge the following afternoon.

When General Grant assumed command of the Union army in the spring of 1864, he appointed Sharpe to his staff. On December 20, 1864, Sharpe was brevetted brigadier general for meritorious service, and on March 13, 1865, brevetted major general and appointed Provost Marshal of the Army of the Potomac. He was present at General Lee's surrender at Appomattox on April 9, 1865, and granted the paroles of the Army of Northern Virginia, including those of Lee and his staff.

Sharpe was mustered out of the army on June 3, 1865. After the war, he filled a number of important U.S. diplomatic and customs posts, and was elected to the New York legislature, where he served as speaker. Sharpe also served on the board of trustees of Rutgers from 1879 until his death on January 13, 1900. He was buried in Wiltwyck Cemetery in Kingston, New York. George H. Sharpe was elected to the Rutgers Hall of Distinguished Alumni in 2006. (Eicher & Eicher, *High Commands*; Fishel, *Secret War*)

Steven D. Glazer

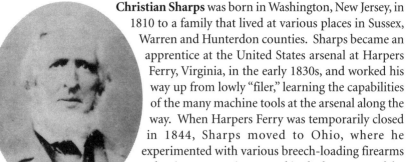

Christian Sharps was born in Washington, New Jersey, in 1810 to a family that lived at various places in Sussex, Warren and Hunterdon counties. Sharps became an apprentice at the United States arsenal at Harpers Ferry, Virginia, in the early 1830s, and worked his way up from lowly "filer," learning the capabilities of the many machine tools at the arsenal along the way. When Harpers Ferry was temporarily closed in 1844, Sharps moved to Ohio, where he experimented with various breech-loading firearms mechanisms, patenting several in the latter part of the decade. In the early 1850s, he established short-term manufacturing relationships to produce his single-shot, lever-action, dropping-breechblock rifle design with A. Nippes at Mill Creek, Pennsylvania, and Robbins and Lawrence in Windsor, Vermont. Investors then joined him in forming the Sharps Rifle Manufacturing Company in Hartford, Connecticut, where Sharps was more involved with sales and distribution than actual product development or production.

**Christian Sharps
(Wayne Browning)**

In 1853, Sharps dissolved all connections with the company that bore his name and formed another corporation, C. Sharps & Company, concentrating on breech-loading pistols. He took William Hankins into partnership early in the Civil War, and the company sold a relatively small number of Sharps & Hankins carbines and rifles, advanced breech loaders chambered for a metallic cartridge, to both the Union army and navy. Meanwhile, the Sharps Rifle Manufacturing Company sold more than 125,000 rifles and carbines of his original design to the Union. Those arms, along with the big buffalo-hunting guns and long-range target rifles the company sold in the postwar period, all stamped with his name, gained Sharps a secure position in the pantheon of American history and folklore.

After the war, Sharps dissolved his partnership with Hankins and resumed making handguns under the C. Sharps & Company name. When Christian Sharps died penniless in Vernon, Connecticut, of tuberculosis on March 12, 1874, his company expired with him. An obituary lamented that he had never received proper compensation for his inventions and described him as one of the "kindest-hearted of men." (Sellers, *Sharps Firearms*)

John W. Kuhl

Timothy E. Shaw, one of Caleb and Christiana Shaw's nine children, was born in Union Township, New Jersey, in 1834, and married Anna Stevens in Camden on February 26, 1856. After inheriting a share of his father's farm, he increased his holdings by buying out his surviving siblings in 1863. When New Jersey authorities, initially reluctant to recruit African-American soldiers, belatedly realized they could shoulder a musket just as well as white men, they extended enlistment bounties to black men like Shaw. When he joined the Union army at Camden on March 22, 1865, Shaw received an $800 Camden County bounty and a $33.33 advance on his $100 federal bounty.

Timothy E. Shaw (Carolyn Williams)

Private Shaw was sent to Camp William Penn outside Philadelphia, and then forwarded as a replacement to the 43rd United States Colored Infantry, which he joined on June 29. The regiment's original ranks were filled by freeborn Pennsylvanians and Jerseymen and newly freed border-state slaves in the spring of 1864. The 43rd was the only regiment to complete its mission successfully at the battle of the Crater on July 30, 1864, when its well-drilled and disciplined men captured 100 Confederate soldiers and an enemy battle flag. By the time Shaw reached the 43rd, the war against the Confederacy was over, but the regiment was stationed in Texas as part of a 50,000-man army intended to threaten French forces supporting Maximilian, the self-styled "emperor" of Mexico.

In the summer of 1865, Timothy Shaw and his comrades patrolled the Rio Grande opposite Matamoras, enduring scorpions, rattlesnakes, malaria, and, when the army supply system broke down, scurvy. Shaw, unimpressed with the regimental surgeon, wrote his wife that he "took the best care I could of myself." Although duty in Texas was unpleasant, literate soldiers in the 43rd established a school to teach their comrades how to read. In the autumn, the regiment returned to Philadelphia, where it was mustered out on November 30.

Timothy Shaw returned to New Jersey and his wife and two sons. In the years following the war, the couple had five more children. In 1880, the family was living on their farm in Centre Township, Camden County. Shaw died of a heart attack on March 10, 1891 and was buried in Blackwood. His widow Anna survived him by a number of years, dying on January 4, 1917. (Bilby, "Timothy Shaw")

Joseph G. Bilby

Alexander D. Snow was born in Connecticut in 1835, but was living in Newark as early as 1850. When he was drafted on May 26, 1864, Snow was a leather worker residing at #15 Wallace Place in Newark. Eventually assigned as a replacement to the 15th New Jersey Infantry's Company B,

A Newark leather factory in the Civil War era. (*Industrial Interests*) Snow arrived at the regiment's camp on September 29. After fighting at Cedar Creek in October, Snow was promoted to corporal on January 1, 1865, and served with the regiment through the siege of Petersburg to the end of the war. When the 15th was mustered out of service in June 1865, Corporal Snow was transferred to the 2nd New Jersey Infantry's Company I and mustered out as a first sergeant with that regiment on July 11, 1865.

Returning to his trade in Newark's patent leather industry as a "Japanner," Snow resided at a series of boarding houses through 1875, when he stopped work due to rheumatism, for which he was granted a $2 monthly pension and treated at the New Jersey Home for Disabled Soldiers. Snow lived at the home from 1877 through 1884. After he left, the ex-sergeant wandered south, through Asbury Park to Point Pleasant, where he worked as a part-time watchman at the Resort House Hotel.

In 1891, Sergeant Snow was admitted to the Morris Plains Asylum suffering from "chronic dementia." One of his delusions was that he had been wounded in several places during the war. According to the doctors, Snow's "prognosis is bad. He will probably die in the hospital." He did, on New Years Day, 1895. He was buried in Fairmount Cemetery in Newark. (Bilby, *Three Rousing Cheers*)

Joseph G. Bilby

David **Southard** was born in Jackson Township, New Jersey, in 1845. When William Halsted received War Department approval to raise an independent regiment of cavalry on August 4, 1861, Southard, a 16-year-old basket maker from the Colliers Mills section of Jackson, was among the first to answer the call for recruits. He arrived in Florence, New Jersey, on August 5, and enlisted as a private in Captain Ivins D. Jones' company, New Jersey Mounted Volunteers, which in six months would become part of the 1st New Jersey Cavalry.

David Southard's grave marker.
(Don Morfe, homeofheroes.com)

By April 1865, Southard, now a sergeant and reenlisted veteran volunteer, was riding with his regiment in rapid pursuit of Lee's retreating army. At the battle of Sailor's Creek on April 6, 1865, Sergeant Southard participated in two charges, the second described as "probably the grandest cavalry charge of the war," where "General Ewell with nearly all of his corps was captured." Southard was conspicuous in this action, and he was recognized in a report by General Henry E. Davies of the First Brigade, Second Cavalry Division as having "[c]aptured a battle flag on the 6th of April 1865, and was afterwards thrown from his horse and the flag taken by an officer of another command. He was the first man that was over the works on the charge made that day." In July, Southard was awarded the Medal of Honor for his heroic actions.

After the war, Southard returned to the pines of Colliers Mills to continue his humble civilian job as a basket maker. In 1892, he became the center of an investigation into the arson fires at several barns owned by Ephraim P. Emson, former freeholder, New Jersey assemblyman and state senator, and at the time current "lay judge" in the Ocean County court system. Emson indicted Southard for the arson, but the veteran vehemently denied the charges, writing to the *New Jersey Courier* in September 1892 that "the only evidence against him [was] that of Peter Wilson, the Negro horsetrader, of Cookstown, who ran the colored camp-meeting (so-called) this summer." Southard claimed he was being "persecuted for political reasons." He was not convicted of any wrongdoing and subsequently died at Pennsylvania Hospital of pneumonia on May 5, 1894. Sergeant Southard was buried in the Zion Baptist Church Cemetery in New Egypt. (Longacre, *Jersey Cavaliers*; MOH citation; *New Jersey Courier*)

Jason Wickersty

Lilly Martin Spencer was born on November 26, 1822, in Exeter, England, as Angelique Marie Martin, the daughter of French teachers who had emigrated from Brittany. The family moved to New York in 1830, and then to Marietta, Ohio, where she took the name Lilly. Although largely self-taught, she also received training from local artists who had attended the Pennsylvania Academy of the Fine Arts. After several successful local shows, she moved to Cincinnati in 1841 and then, following her 1844 marriage to Benjamin Rush Spencer, a tailor who gave up his own work to assist her, to New York, where she thought her career would advance more rapidly. In between having children – she gave birth to thirteen, seven surviving to adulthood — Spencer exhibited at the National Academy of Design and became an honorary member of the National Academy.

Lilly Martin Spencer
(Wickimedia Commons)

In 1858, the Spencers moved to Newark, New Jersey, where she rented a studio at 461 High Street, in a building owned by **Marcus L. Ward**. Reportedly in exchange for part of her studio rent, she painted a family portrait, *The Four Children of Marcus Ward*, for the future New Jersey governor. Spencer became famous for her "domestic scenes," and with the outbreak of the Civil War merged her genre with the history unfolding around her, most notably in her 1866 work, *War Spirit at Home: Celebrating the Battle of Vicksburg*, which portrays a mother scanning the war news in a newspaper while her children march around the room in imitation of a military parade. The painting first went on display at Campbell's framing shop in Newark. Spencer used several of her own children as models for *War Spirit*, which is currently part of the Newark Museum collection.

Although she did not become wealthy as an artist, Spencer was perhaps the most famous American woman painter of the time. In 1876 she received a gold medal at the Philadelphia Centennial Exposition. She moved to Highland, New York, in 1879, but her time in Newark is considered her most prolific period. Spencer worked up to the day she died, May 22, 1902, passing away at her easel. She is buried beside her husband in Highland. (Lurie & Mappen, *Encyclopedia of New Jersey;* Holzer and Neely, *Mine Eyes Have Seen the Glory*)

Joseph G. Bilby

William Spencer was born in New Jersey on September 16, 1823 and served in the 10ᵗʰ U.S. Infantry in the Mexican War of 1846-1848, enlisting in that regiment in April 1847. Spencer married Susan Case in 1848 and was living in Stanhope in September 1862 when he reentered the service, joining the 27ᵗʰ New Jersey Infantry for a nine-month enlistment. He was mustered out in June 1863 and, not having two years of service in the Civil War, found himself subject to the draft. Spencer was conscripted on June 2, 1864, and assigned to Company H of the 15ᵗʰ New Jersey Infantry. He joined his new regiment on August 23 and was shot in the left hip at the battle of Winchester on September 19. Sent to Ward Hospital in Newark to recuperate, Spencer and other New Jersey soldiers recuperating there were furloughed home in November in hopes they would vote for Abraham Lincoln, since New Jersey did not allow soldiers to vote by absentee ballot.

(Frederich Otto, findagrave.com)

Upon his return to the 15ᵗʰ New Jersey in February 1865, Spencer was detailed to the Quartermaster Department and served there for the rest of the war. When his regiment was mustered out, Private Spencer was transferred to the 2ⁿᵈ New Jersey Infantry and discharged with that regiment on July 11, 1865. After the war he lived in Roxbury Township with his wife and four children, working as a farm laborer.

In 1887, Spencer marshaled several other veterans of the 15ᵗʰ, including Ezekial Rarick of Company F and Mount Olive, as witnesses for his disability pension application. The old soldier, veteran of four regiments and two wars, died on May 7, 1899, and was buried in the Presbyterian/Methodist-Episcopal Cemetery in Succasunna. (Bilby, *Three Rousing Cheers*)

William Spencer's grave marker does not list all the units he served in. (Frederich Otto, findagrave.com)

Joseph G. Bilby

Rebecca Buffum Spring was born in Rhode Island on June 8, 1811, to a strongly abolitionist Quaker family. A progressive reformer from her earliest days, Spring was educated at the Smithfield Academy in Fall River, Massachusetts, and worked teaching mill children at factory schools in Massachusetts and Philadelphia. She married Marcus Spring, a wealthy Philadelphia merchant, in 1836. The couple had three children and a strong and loving egalitarian marriage in an era when such relationships were considered a rarity.

Rebecca Buffum Spring
(Macpherson Collection,
Scripps College)

The idealistic Springs were friends of many leading intellectuals and social reformers of the day, which led them to New Jersey and financial participation and leadership roles in two experimental communities, the North American Phalanx near Red Bank, from 1843 to 1855, and Perth Amboy's Raritan Bay Union, from 1853 to 1858. Spring taught at the Union's coeducational Eagleswood School, where she and her husband sponsored a lecture series featuring leading cultural icons of the day, including Henry David Thoreau and Ralph Waldo Emerson. Spring was, however, first and foremost, an abolitionist. Eagleswood, with a teaching

Raritan Bay Union and Eagleswood School in 1858.
(*Frank Leslie's Illustrated Newspaper*)

staff that included **Sarah Moore Grimké**, also served as an Underground Railroad Station. Spring visited John Brown in prison following his abortive raid on Harpers Ferry, and two of Brown's men were buried on Raritan Bay Union property.

Following the outbreak of the Civil War, Spring and her husband established a school for slave children in Norfolk, Virginia, and fed and clothed escaped slaves making their way north. Although a deeply religious pacifist herself, Spring thought a Union victory so important that she allowed the Eagleswood School to become a military academy for the duration of the war. Before the Raritan Bay Union ceased to exist in 1868, the Springs also established a highly regarded artists' colony on the property.

When her husband died in 1874, Spring moved to Los Angeles, California, where she continued her involvement in progressive causes, including the women's suffrage movement. Rebecca Buffum Spring, a notable prototype of modern feminism, died in Los Angeles at the age of 99 on February 8, 1911. (Lurie & Mappen, *Encyclopedia of New Jersey*; Lurie, *A New Jersey Anthology*; Switala, *Underground Railroad*)

Joseph G. Bilby

Hazard Stanford was born in Georgia in 1844 and enlisted in the Union army at Camden, New Jersey, as a substitute for draftee Alexander McCray of Cape May, on July 19, 1864. Stanford was handed an envelope containing $10 of his substitute fee by Provost Marshal Alexander Wentz and transported under guard to the Trenton draft and recruit rendezvous, where he would receive the rest of his money and be forwarded to a New Jersey unit in the field.

Stanford was no stranger to uniforms. Despite his youth, he had fought in the battle of Olustee, Florida, in January and had left the lines at Bermuda Hundred in Virginia just three days prior to his enlistment at Camden. He had deserted from the 64th Georgia Infantry, Confederate States Army, five days prior to that. On August 23, when Stanford arrived at the camp of his new

Confederate deserters coming into Union lines, as Stanford did. (*Harper's Weekly*)

unit, the 15th New Jersey Infantry, then campaigning in Virginia's Shenandoah Valley, he made no secret of his prior affiliation, stating he was from Lumpkin County, Georgia, and that his father was a Confederate colonel. His new comrades bore him no ill will.

Hazard Stanford fought with the 15th in the battle of Winchester in September, where he was wounded in the ankle, entered the casualty evacuation chain and ended up at Satterlee General Hospital in West Philadelphia, Pennsylvania, from where he received a disability discharge on June 14, 1865. Although Stanford told hospital personnel he was going back to Camden, the temporary Jerseyman limped out of Satterlee and into a void. Attempts to find him through pension and census records, as well as city and county directories for Georgia, New Jersey and Pennsylvania, have proved fruitless. His date of death is unknown. (Bilby, *Three Rousing Cheers*)

Joseph G. Bilby

William Still was born on November 21, 1821, the youngest of eighteen children of escaped slave Charity Still and her husband, Levin, a former slave who had purchased his own freedom. Originally from the Eastern Shore of Maryland, the Stills settled in southern New Jersey, eventually living in Medford, Burlington County, where William Still was born and spent his youth. A farmer, Still had little formal education, but moved to Philadelphia in 1844, where he was hired as a clerk by the Pennsylvania Society for the Abolition of Slavery. Recognizing his organizational skills, the society appointed him chairman of a committee established to aid runaway slaves reaching Philadelphia. Still

William Still (Library of Congress)

subsequently rose rapidly in the abolitionist movement, establishing friendships within its leadership, including Frederick Douglass and John Brown. As a conductor on the Underground Railroad, he also worked closely with **Harriet Tubman**. His book, *The Underground Railroad: A Record of Facts, Authentic Narratives, Letters, etc.*, published in 1872, is considered perhaps the most important reference on that institution.

Still became not only a leader in the abolitionist movement, but also a spokesman for Philadelphia's African-American community, leading the struggle to desegregate the city's public transit system in the pre-Civil War period. An astute businessman as well, he became a successful coal merchant. Still was also post sutler at Camp William Penn, where African-American regiments were organized during the Civil War. His brother was James Still, the famed "Black Doctor of the [New Jersey] Pine Barrens." William Still married Letitia George in 1847 and the couple had four children who survived to adulthood, including Caroline, an early female doctor who graduated from the Women's Medical College of Philadelphia. William Still died on July 14, 1902. He is buried in Eden Memorial Cemetery, Collingdale, Pennsylvania. (Bethel, *African-American Identity*; Lurie & Mappen, *Encyclopedia of New Jersey*; Still, *Underground Railroad*; Switala, *Underground Railroad*)

Joseph G. Bilby

James Sherwin Stratton (John W. Kuhl)

James Sherwin Stratton was born in Mullica Hill, New Jersey, in 1843, the son of New Jersey Congressman Nathan T. Stratton, who often brought him to Washington when Congress was in session, providing the young man with aspirations to eventually follow in the elder Stratton's footsteps. On one such trip, he had the opportunity to meet Abraham Lincoln. Stratton enlisted as a sergeant in the 12th New Jersey Infantry in September 1862. He was promoted to second lieutenant of the regiment's Company F on June 23, 1863, replacing Second Lieutenant Joseph Pierson, who was lost at Chancellorsville.

Lieutenant Stratton was detailed to Trenton on recruiting service in May of 1864 and shortly afterwards rejoined the 12th with a promotion to first lieutenant. As commander of Company K, he participated bravely with his men throughout the Petersburg Campaign until he was killed in action at the age of twenty-one while leading an ill-fated charge at Reams Station, Virginia, on August 25. Lieutenant Stratton's body was hastily buried on the field, but his grave was marked. His father and his brother, Captain Edward Stratton, obtained permission to recover the remains in the summer of 1865 and brought his body home for burial in the Baptist Church Cemetery in Mullica Hill. (Bilby, *Remember You Are Jerseymen*)

Richard Mendoza

The Battle of Reams Station
(*Frank Leslie's Illustrated Newspaper*)

William Scudder Stryker was born in Trenton on June 6, 1838, and graduated from Princeton in 1858. In April 1861, he enlisted as a private in "A Company, New Jersey National Guard Infantry," a militia organization called up by Governor **Charles Olden** to protect the state arsenal, and was mustered out after three months. In the summer of 1862, Stryker was appointed a major by Governor **Joel Parker** and assigned as disbursing and quartermaster officer at Freehold's Camp Vredenburgh, where he helped organize the 14th New Jersey Infantry.

In February 1863, Stryker was commissioned a major and paymaster of U. S. Volunteers, assigned to Hilton Head, South Carolina. As a member of General Quincy Gillmore's staff, he participated in the siege of Charleston, including the disastrous July 18 attack on Battery Wagner. After that fierce fight, Major Stryker visited the survivors of the 54th Massachusetts Infantry in a successful search for Henry D. Wood, an African-American soldier from Trenton. Stryker was later transferred to the Columbus, Ohio, Parole Camp, and served as senior paymaster until June 30, 1866, when he resigned as a brevet lieutenant colonel, a rank he received for meritorious service.

William Scudder Stryker (John W. Kuhl)

On April 12, 1867, Governor **Marcus Ward** commissioned Stryker a brigadier general and appointed him New Jersey's adjutant general, in charge of the state's military administration, a post he held for the rest of his life. In 1870, Stryker married Helen Boudinot Atterbury. The couple had three children. He was brevetted major general during Governor **Joel Parker**'s second term in 1874.

His thirty-three years in office made Stryker the longest serving adjutant general in New Jersey history, but he is best known for his work as a historian. His assiduous attention to detail in compiling lists of Jerseymen who served in the nation's wars resulted in publications that remain standard references today, and no one can write a complete New Jersey military history without consulting his numerous books and articles, rich with primary source material, on the state's role in the American Revolution. As a member and officer of many American and European historical societies, including a term as president of the New Jersey Historical Society, Stryker's contributions to New Jersey historiography were enormous. When he died in Trenton on October 29, 1900, William Stryker was remembered as "modest and unassuming beyond most men." His accomplishments certainly spoke for him. General Stryker is buried in Trenton's Riverview Cemetery. (Bilby & Goble, *Remember You Are Jerseymen*; Luzky, *Adjutants General of NJ*)

Joseph G. Bilby

George William Taylor (John W. Kuhl)

George William Taylor was born November 22, 1808, in High Bridge, New Jersey, the son of iron mine owner Archibald Taylor. Taylor graduated from Alden Partridge's Connecticut military academy, served four years as a navy midshipman and then went to work in the family business. During the Mexican War he helped enlist a company of the 10th U.S. Infantry, a regular army regiment largely recruited in New Jersey, and was commissioned a lieutenant in March 1847. Taylor was promoted to captain during his service, left the army at the end of the war, and spent three years in Gold Rush-era California before returning home.

Taylor was appointed colonel of the 3rd New Jersey Infantry in June 1861. The 3rd was part of General **Philip Kearny**'s First New Jersey Brigade, and when Kearny was elevated to division command, Taylor was promoted to brigadier general and brigade command. He led the Jerseymen through the Peninsula Campaign. At Gaines' Mill, on June 27, 1862, the brigade's regiments were committed to the fight piecemeal and the Union line was overrun. Showing great personal valor, Taylor rallied his men to establish a second defensive line, helping to save the Union forces from complete disaster. The brigade then retreated to Harrison's Landing with the rest of the federal army.

In August 1862, Taylor's brigade was sent to northern Virginia to reinforce General John Pope's beleaguered army. Ordered to Manassas Junction, the Jerseyans detrained at Bull Run Bridge on the morning of August 27. The general, characterized as "a brave, but not over prudent man" by one of his soldiers, had no idea what was to his front, but advanced anyway. Unfortunately, he encountered "Stonewall" Jackson's entire army corps. As the Jersey Brigade advanced into heavy artillery fire, Rebel cavalry began to infiltrate its rear area. Suddenly realizing his situation, Taylor ordered a retreat, which began in an orderly manner, then deteriorated, although most of the Jerseymen successfully escaped the enemy trap.

During the withdrawal, Taylor was wounded in the leg by a shell fragment and evacuated to an Alexandria hospital, where he died of his wounds on August 31. Hundreds of people turned out for General Taylor's funeral and burial at the Presbyterian Church Cemetery in Clinton, where an impressive monument still stands as a testimonial to his sacrifice, if not his prudence. (Bilby & Goble, *Remember You Are Jerseymen*; Kuhl, "General George William Taylor"; Brown Memoir)

Thomas R. Burke Jr.

James C. Taylor was born in 1842 in Lambertville, New Jersey, and was living in the Mill Hill section of Trenton when he enlisted as a corporal in Company B of the 14th New Jersey Infantry in August of 1862. Taylor's father, James Sr., was a mortician who "…made a lot of money by his invention of a convenient body cooler…"

Taylor was reduced in rank to private for some unknown infraction in October 1863. Although hospitalized for illness during brief periods over the next two years, he took part in all his regiment's battles through Monocacy, where on July 9, 1864, he was captured in the wake of a Confederate assault

James C. Taylor (John W. Kuhl)

that overwhelmed the Union line. Originally reported as "missing in action," Taylor's fate was clarified when a scrap of paper bearing his signature was discovered amidst the battlefield detritus. The hastily scrawled note, later published in the *Trenton True American*, conveyed his status as a prisoner of war to the home folks. After spending seven months in a POW camp at Danville, Virginia, Taylor, in ill health due to his captivity, was exchanged in February 1865.

After the war, apparently unaffected by the harvest of death he had witnessed, Taylor followed in his father's footsteps and became an undertaker. He also became prominent in veterans' affairs as a member of Trenton's Aaron Wilkes GAR Post #23. Taylor served a term in the New Jersey assembly in 1886, taking the opportunity to snip a swatch off of each of the New Jersey battle flags displayed in the state house. Although this practice would horrify a modern historical conservator, it was part and parcel of Victorian sentimentality, and Taylor framed the flag fragments for posterity.

Lucky in war, James Taylor was not so fortunate in his postwar private life. His wife and three of his four sons predeceased him. He died on January 30, 1904, and was buried in Riverview Cemetery in Trenton. (Martin, *The Monocacy Regiment*)

Postwar photograph of James C. Taylor. (John W. Kuhl)

Joseph G. Bilby

George W. Thompson was born in New Jersey in 1843. Thompson was working as a miller when he joined the 15th New Jersey Infantry's Company E on August 12, 1862. He served with the company until May 8, 1864, when he was hit in the left elbow by a bullet as the 15th was driven off of Laurel Hill at Spotsylvania. Thompson's arm was bandaged at the regimental aid station, but his wound was not thoroughly examined until he reached Finlay Hospital in Washington, DC, on May 11. Although Surgeon G. L. Pancoast found Thompson's elbow joint shattered beyond repair, he

George W. Thompson (John W. Kuhl)

did not amputate. Instead, Pancoast removed the joint and other damaged bone, leaving the arm externally intact but essentially useless and two-inches shorter. Thompson's excised elbow joint was presented to the United States Army Medical Museum and is currently part of the Armed Forces Pathological Institute collection.

George W. Thompson (John W. Kuhl)

Discharged from the army as "totally unfit" in February 1865, Thompson returned to New Jersey with a pension of $18 a month. No longer able to ply the miller's trade, the disabled veteran worked for a while as a book canvasser and then opened a small store in Trenton selling lamps and gasoline. After a stint as an assistant keeper at the state prison, he went to work as a salesman for his brother's gristmill.

On May 23, 1870, Thompson married Mary E. Phares. The couple had four children. Very active in veterans' affairs, he was a member of Aaron Wilkes GAR Post #23 in Trenton. The old veteran died on February 26, 1915, and was buried in Riverview Cemetery in Trenton. (Bilby, *Three Rousing Cheers*)

Joseph G. Bilby

John James Toffey was born in Pawling, New York, on June 1, 1844. In September of 1862, he enlisted in the 21st New Jersey Infantry and served with that regiment until it was mustered out of service in June of 1863. Toffey then volunteered for the 33rd New Jersey Infantry, organizing at Newark's Camp Frelinghuysen, and was commissioned a first lieutenant.

On November 23, 1863, the 33rd was heavily engaged with Confederate forces at Citico Creek near Chattanooga, Tennessee, as Union forces began to raise the siege of that beleaguered city. When another officer was mortally wounded, Toffey was ordered forward to take his place. After running a gauntlet where "bullets flew like hailstones," Toffey arrived at the position only to be severely wounded in the hip. Evacuated to a hospital, Lieutenant Toffey survived his wound, but was unable to return to active duty. Some 34 years later, he would be awarded the Medal of Honor for distinguished gallantry for his actions at Citico Creek.

John James Toffey
(John W. Kuhl)

After convalescing, Toffey was transferred to the Veteran Reserve Corps in Washington, D.C., and was present at Ford's Theatre the night President Abraham Lincoln was shot. Back home in Jersey City after the war, he became active in the livestock business and Republican politics. Toffey held public office as a Jersey City alderman, Hudson County sheriff and New Jersey state treasurer, among other positions. He was also active in the New Jersey National Guard and the GAR. He died in Jersey City on March 13, 1911 and was buried in Pawling, New York. (J. Toffey Papers; Zinn, *The Mutinous Regiment*)

John Zinn

John James Toffey
(New Jersey State Archives)

John Trembly was born in 1834. He married a woman from Rahway, and the Trembly family moved south before the Civil War. The family was living in Georgia at the outbreak of the conflict. Family tradition related in Trembly's obituary held that while his wife and children returned to Rahway, he was drafted into the Confederate army, although this may not have happened right away, since the Confederacy did not begin drafting men until the spring of 1862. It is also possible that Trembly joined the Confederate army for his own safety, considering his Yankee origins. Although there is no record of his Southern service, many Confederate records did not survive the war. Names similar to Trembly's do appear, however, on several Georgia rosters.

In 1862, Trembly reportedly deserted from the Confederate army and promptly enlisted in Company D of the Union army's 10th Tennessee Volunteers, and does appear on the roster of that unit. The 10th spent most of its service on prisoner and railroad guard duty and in counter-guerilla operations in Tennessee, but was never in an actual battle. After his discharge, Trembly returned to Rahway,

John Trembly's grave marker. (Diane C. MacAvoy)

where he lived for the rest of his life. According to his obituary, he was barred from joining the primary Union veterans' organization, the GAR, because, even though he was a pensioned Union veteran, he had once borne arms against the United States, however unwillingly. Trembly died on April 28, 1907, and is buried in Rahway Cemetery. (Eckhardt & MacAvoy, *Our Brothers Gone Before*; *NY Times* Obituary).

Robert F. MacAvoy

Lorenzo Dowd Trent, an African-American, was born in 1849 in an area of Virginia that later became West Virginia, and was orphaned prior to the outbreak of the Civil War. In late July of 1863, the 13th New Jersey Infantry, a unit recruited in the state's urban northeast, arrived in Harpers Ferry. When Trent wandered into camp, the Jerseymen adopted the genial young man as a regimental "aide." He soldiered along with the regiment for the rest of the war, as the 13th went west and fought at Chattanooga and then with General William T. Sherman to Atlanta, the March to the Sea and into the Carolinas. The regiment finished the war in Washington, DC, where, after the Grand Review and muster-out, Trent returned to New Jersey with his new "family."

Lorenzo Dowd Trent driving Chief Carhuff to a fire in the 1870s. (*Newark Fire History*)

By 1867, Lorenzo Trent was living in Newark and working for the city's fire department, a mixed volunteer and professional organization, as a stable hand and groom. Trent gained a reputation as an industrious and reliable worker, and when Ellis R. Carhuff was appointed chief engineer of the department and decided to respond to fires on horseback, he requested that Trent be assigned to personally care for his mount. In 1871, the Newark city council purchased a horse-drawn two-wheel carriage or "gig" for the chief engineer's use, and Carhuff requested Trent as his driver. Trent soon became well known all over Newark, as whenever a fire alarm sounded, one of the first pieces of equipment to arrive on the scene was Carhuff's gig, with Trent in the driver's seat. Over the years, Trent also became an ordained Methodist deacon, and was married and divorced. In 1880, he was living with his seven-year-old son Harry and three-year-old daughter Nellie and seventy-year-old housekeeper Rebecca Steward.

Unfortunately, on Sunday January 9, 1881, Lorenzo Trent answered his last alarm, to a chimney fire at 76 Liberty Street. On the way back to headquarters he became ill and Chief Carhuff personally brought him home. When Trent's condition deteriorated, he was hospitalized and diagnosed with meningitis. He died on January 21 and was buried from Saint John's Methodist Episcopal Church, his last rites conducted by three ministers and attended by an "overflowing crowd." He was buried at Evergreen Cemetery in Hillside. (http://www.newarkfirehistory.com/)

Thomas R. Burke Jr.

William Snyder Truex was born on October 2, 1819, in the New Monmouth section of Middletown. He enrolled at the United States Military Academy at West Point in 1837 but left after one year. Truex enlisted in the 10th U.S. Infantry in March 1847 during the Mexican War and rose from private to first lieutenant before his discharge in August 1848. With the outbreak of the Civil War, his military experience earned him the rank of major in the 5th New Jersey Infantry. In March of 1862, when the disorganized "Olden Legion" was transferred to state control as the 10th New Jersey Infantry, Truex was transferred to the unit as lieutenant colonel, and when the 14th New Jersey Infantry was formed in July, he was appointed its colonel.

William Snyder Truex
(New Jersey State Archives)

The 14th, recruited from Monmouth, Ocean, Mercer, Middlesex and Union counties, left Freehold's Camp Vredenburgh in September 1862, and spent the next ten months at Frederick, Maryland, guarding the Monocacy River railroad junction. After Gettysburg, the 14th was ordered to the Army of the Potomac, where it was assigned to the Third Army Corps and engaged in its first fight at Locust Grove, Virginia, in November, losing 16 men killed and 58 wounded.

In the spring of 1864, the 14th was transferred to the Sixth Corps and Colonel Truex advanced to brigade command. Truex was slightly wounded in the hand on May 31 at Hanover Court House, Virginia, and his old regiment suffered severely at Cold Harbor the following day, losing one third of its men in two hours. Fighting across their old garrison grounds at Monocacy on July 9, 1864, Truex and his men delayed a Confederate raid towards Washington for a crucial day, saving the capital from possible enemy capture. In the aftermath of the battle, however, Truex squabbled with division commander General James B. Ricketts over bringing his horse onto a railroad boxcar, left the army without authorization and went home. As a result, despite his outstanding combat record, he was court-martialed in absentia and dismissed from the army. The problem was eventually resolved and Truex returned to duty to be mustered out of the service a brevet brigadier general in June 1865. He died in Trenton on September 5, 1889, and was buried in the city's Riverview Cemetery. (Martin, *The Monocacy Regiment*)

Thomas R. Burke Jr.

Harriet Ross Tubman, famed Underground Railroad conductor, was a frequent visitor to and part-time resident of New Jersey. Born a slave circa 1820 in Maryland, Tubman married free African-American John Tubman in 1844. The marriage ended five years later following her escape from slavery.

Once free, Tubman spent the rest of her life helping to free other slaves through the Underground Railroad and abolitionist movements. She is credited with personally leading over 300 slaves to freedom, an effort that gained her the nickname "Black Moses." In order to finance her anti-slavery activities, Tubman worked as a hotel cook in the New Jersey shore resort of Cape May during the summers of 1849 through 1852, and helped establish the "Southern Network" of the state's Underground Railroad during that period. During the Civil War, she returned south to assist Union forces as a spy and guide. In 1864,

Harriet Ross Tubman
(National Park Service)

Tubman visited Camp William Penn, a training camp for black Union soldiers, including many from New Jersey, and delivered a morale-boosting address to the troops in a rousing "down-home" manner.

After the war, Tubman remarried and moved to Auburn, New York, where she and her new husband, Nelson Davis, opened a refuge for homeless African-Americans. Abolitionist leader and New Jerseyan **William Still** wrote that although "a woman of no pretensions," Tubman was, "in point of courage, shrewdness, and disinterested exertions to rescue her fellow men," indeed "without…equal." Harriet Tubman Davis died on March 10, 1913. She was buried with military honors at Fort Hill Cemetery in Auburn and a Liberty Ship was named after her during World War II. (Lurie & Mappen, *Encyclopedia of New Jersey;* Scott, *Camp William Penn*)

Joseph G. Bilby

James Beatty Turner was born in 1835 in Ardee, County Louth, Ireland, and received his early education at King's Court, County Cavan. He immigrated with his family to New York City in 1849 and subsequently settled in Jersey City. Turner graduated from New York University Law School with honors, was admitted to the New York Bar in 1859 and practiced law in the city until the outbreak of the Civil War.

In April 1861, Turner enlisted as a private in Company C of the 2nd New Jersey Militia. While serving his three-month enlistment, he wrote a series of letters on the 2nd's activities that were published in New York's *Irish American* newspaper under the pen name "Jersey Blue." On the formation of the Irish Brigade in the fall of 1861, Turner was commissioned a first lieutenant in the brigade's 88th New York Infantry, but was informally assigned to brigade commander General Thomas Francis Meagher's staff. Meagher, a charismatic and romantic figure, was looking for a writer to provide a public chronicle of his brigade's deeds, and the publisher of the *Irish American* recommended Turner, who gained the unofficial title "Bard of the Irish Brigade."

Using the *nom de plume* "Gallowglass," after the Scottish warriors employed by medieval Irish lords, as a reminder of his commitment to Irish independence, Turner dramatically chronicled the marches and battles of the Irish Brigade in the pages of the *Irish American* until he was severely wounded in the left arm at the battle of Antietam in September 1862.

Sunken road at Antietam where James Beatty Turner was wounded. (Library of Congress)

Turner returned to Jersey City to convalesce, and married his neighborhood sweetheart, Annie McNamara. In February 1863, he was promoted to captain and appointed assistant adjutant general of the Irish Brigade, although he was not well enough to rejoin the brigade until April 1864. On May 5, 1864, while accompanying brigade commander Colonel Thomas A. Smyth in the battle of the Wilderness, Turner was shot in the head and instantly killed. He left behind his wife and an infant daughter, and was buried in Bayview - New York Bay Cemetery in Jersey City. (Bilby, *Remember Fontenoy*)

James M. Madden

Edwin D. Ulmer (John W. Kuhl)

Edwin D. Ulmer was born in Hunterdon County, New Jersey, in 1842 and enlisted in the 15th New Jersey Infantry's Company G as a corporal in August 1862. He was promoted to sergeant on June 1, 1864, and first sergeant on October 1, 1864. Ulmer served with the regiment until he was wounded in the left leg and fell to the ground at the battle of Cedar Creek on October 19, 1864, as the regiment was retreating to a better defensive position. Bypassed by advancing Confederate soldiers who took his wallet, Ulmer was saved from captivity when Union forces counterattacked and won the day. Nine hours after he was wounded, he was discovered by stretcher bearers and brought to a field hospital.

Sergeant Ulmer was eventually transported to Jarvis Hospital in Baltimore. Surgeons there tried to save his leg, but blood poisoning set in and it was amputated at mid-thigh on November 24. A loose piece of bone was removed in March 1865, and the sergeant's condition was deemed sufficiently satisfactory to release him from the hospital and the army on May 29. On his way home to New Jersey, however, Ulmer was knocked down by a running child in a railway station, an accident that reopened the wound and left him in a weakened condition.

Ulmer's recovery was slow and dogged by setbacks. His wound reopened again in 1866 and he was diagnosed with osteomyelitis. In yet another operation his stump was amputated further up, and his badly diseased hip joint was removed. The sergeant was one of only eight Civil War soldiers to survive this surgical procedure known as "resection," which earned him an entry in *The Medical and Surgical History of the War of the Rebellion.*

Ulmer after hip surgery. (John W. Kuhl)

Ulmer lived as normal a life as possible, considering his disability. In the postwar years he married and lived in both Philadelphia, where he worked as a clerk and bookkeeper, and Milford, New Jersey, where he was a telegraph operator. He and his wife had three children, Frank, Margaret and Annie. Sergeant Ulmer died in 1891 of "paralysis" and was buried in the Milford Union Cemetery. (Bilby, *Three Rousing Cheers*)

Joseph G. Bilby

Alexander Arsace Vandoni was born in Italy on January 29, 1833, and immigrated to the United States in 1850. In 1861, he was living in the East Madison section of Chatham Township as a self-employed broom and brush maker. Although profits were small, Vandoni was able to support himself and his wife, Annie Ryan, an Irish girl he married on July 9, 1861.

In the summer of 1862, the New Jersey Adjutant General called for the state's troop quota of 10,478 men for nine-months service to either volunteer or be drafted by September 1. Vandoni answered the call, enlisting as a musician in Company E of the 27th New Jersey Infantry, organized at Newark's Camp Frelinghuysen. The regiment left Newark on October 10, and, after several weeks of drill in Washington, joined the Army of the Potomac's Ninth Army Corps.

Alexander Arsace Vandoni's grave marker. (Barbara Schaffer, findagrave.com)

The 27th was held in reserve during the battle of Fredericksburg in December, and Vandoni poked around in the town's wreckage for war souvenirs. In February 1863, the regiment left its winter quarters at Falmouth for Newport News, Virginia, at the outset of a journey that would make it one of the most traveled New Jersey Civil War units. In March, the 27th moved on to Cincinnati and then down into Kentucky. On May 5, the regiment lost 33 men, 19 of them from Rockaway Township, who drowned in the largest single non-combat casualty incident for New Jerseyans in the war, when a flatboat crossing the Cumberland River overturned. On the way home in June, the regiment paused near Pittsburgh for possible service repulsing the Confederate invasion of Pennsylvania. Unneeded, the Jerseyans proceeded to Newark, where they were mustered out of service on July 2, 1863.

His military adventure over, Alexander Vandoni returned to the quiet life of a broom maker, his family income eventually supplemented by his wife's earnings as a nurse and his daughter Orletta's dressmaking business. He never missed a reunion of the 27th's veterans, and every July 4th would put on his GAR uniform, sling his drum, stand on his lawn, and rattle away to his heart's content, remembering the way it was back in '62 and '63. He died on February 29, 1908, and was buried in the Hancock Cemetery in Florham Park. (Bilby & Goble, *Remember You Are Jerseymen*; Vandoni Diary)

Joseph G. Bilby

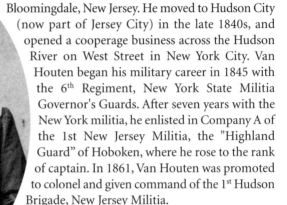

Gilliam Van Houten was born August 30, 1819, in Bloomingdale, New Jersey. He moved to Hudson City (now part of Jersey City) in the late 1840s, and opened a cooperage business across the Hudson River on West Street in New York City. Van Houten began his military career in 1845 with the 6th Regiment, New York State Militia Governor's Guards. After seven years with the New York militia, he enlisted in Company A of the 1st New Jersey Militia, the "Highland Guard" of Hoboken, where he rose to the rank of captain. In 1861, Van Houten was promoted to colonel and given command of the 1st Hudson Brigade, New Jersey Militia.

In addition to his militia experience, Van Houten was very active in civil affairs in Hudson County. His public service included terms as Director of the Hudson County Board of Freeholders, Hoboken alderman, Hudson City alderman and president of the Hudson City Board of Education.

Gilliam Van Houten
(James M. Madden)

Van Houten helped recruit and train the first troops organized in Trenton under President Lincoln's call for militia volunteers to defend Washington, and according to the *American Standard* newspaper, was rumored to be Governor **Charles Olden's** first choice to serve as colonel of the 1st New Jersey Militia in 1861. Van Houten returned to Hudson City, however, where he was subsequently appointed colonel of the 21st New Jersey Volunteer Infantry, recruited in the summer of 1862 for nine-months service. After reaching the Army of the Potomac in Virginia, the 21st was attached to the Third Brigade of the Second Division of the Sixth Army Corps.

On May 4, 1863, in a fight at Salem Heights, Virginia, during the Chancellorsville Campaign, the 21st was overrun by a Confederate attack. Colonel Van Houten, who tried to rally his men, was severely wounded in his right leg and died the following day at a field hospital under enemy control. His body was recovered under a flag of truce and returned to New Jersey, where he was buried in his family cemetery in Franklin Lakes. GAR Post #3 in Jersey City was named in his honor. (Bilby & Goble, *Remember You Are Jerseymen*)

James M. Madden

Peter Vredenburgh Jr. was born in Freehold, New Jersey, on September 12, 1837. The son of a prominent Monmouth County judge, he was inclined towards law and was a practicing attorney in New York City when the Civil War broke out.

On August 25, 1862, Vredenburgh was commissioned as major of the 14th New Jersey Infantry. The 14th was mustered into service at Camp Vredenburgh, located on the old Revolutionary War Monmouth battlefield and named after the major's father. In early 1863, when the regiment was detailed to guard the Monocacy River railroad junction near Frederick, Maryland, Vredenburgh became

Peter Vredenburgh Jr. (Andrew M. Megill)

provost marshall of the city of Frederick, where his legal and administrative skills were put to good use. He was subsequently appointed inspector general of the Third Division of the Third Army Corps and then the entire Third Corps. When the Third Corps was disbanded in March of 1864, Major Vredenburgh was assigned to the Sixth Corps staff. In the late summer of 1864, he petitioned to return to his old regiment, which had suffered heavy casualties that year, including at the crucial battle of Monocacy in July, critically delaying a Confederate force marching on Washington.

An early postwar photo of Opequon Creek, Virginia, crossed by Peter Vredenburgh Jr. and the 14th NJ on September 19, 1864. He was killed soon afterward. (USAMHI)

On September 10, Vredenburgh assumed command of the 14th. As he led the regiment into the battle of Opequon or Third Winchester, Virginia, on September 19, Vredenburgh turned to his troops and said, "I'll do all I can for you boys." Turning to face front, he was hit in the throat by an unexploded three-inch artillery shell and killed instantly. Vredenburgh's body was returned to New Jersey and buried at Maplewood Cemetery in Freehold. The major's frock coat is currently on display in the Monocacy Battlefield Visitor Center near Frederick, Maryland, and his letters are in the collection of the Monmouth County Historical Society. (Martin, *The Monocacy Regiment*)

Thomas R. Burke Jr.

James Walter Wall was born in Trenton on May 26, 1820, the son of prominent New Jersey politician and U. S. Senator Garret Dorset Wall. After graduating from Princeton, he studied law and was admitted to the bar in 1841. Wall moved to Burlington, New Jersey, in 1847 and was elected mayor there in 1850. After declining a Democratic Party nomination for Congress in 1850, he ran unsuccessfully for a congressional seat in 1854.

James Walter Wall (Library of Congress)

Wall attended the 1860 Democratic convention in Charleston as a New Jersey delegate and supporter of Southern candidate Vice President James C. Breckinridge. An outspoken critic of the Union cause from the very outset of the war, he wrote inflammatory articles in copperhead newspapers. On September 11, 1861, Wall was dragged kicking and screaming out of his house by a posse of U. S. marshals and Burlington police. He went down hard, tossing one officer across the room and knocking another unconscious. Never formally charged, Wall was offered release after two weeks upon signing a loyalty oath and quickly complied, but later complained bitterly of "the wrong and outrage" inflicted upon him by the government. At home, he proclaimed himself "armed to the teeth," and threatened that another incident would result in "a dead marshal on my doorstep."

Following the death of New Jersey U.S. Senator John R. Thomson in office in 1863, Wall was elected by the state's legislature to fill out the six-week remainder of Thomson's term, even though his extremism did not reflect the mainstream party view. Historian William Gillette has characterized Wall's mini-term as "brief and insignificant," and he was replaced by wealthy Newark harness manufacturer William Wright, a less polarizing choice.

Dismissing the moral issue of human slavery, Wall, like many copperheads, chose to characterize it as a local private-property issue viewed through a lens of inherently racist assumptions. During his brief senate tenure, he posited that abolition would result in "a white nation, which lost its liberties and its name in endeavoring to give freedom to the black and inferior race."

After his brief and bombastic strut across the national stage, James W. Wall returned to relative obscurity and the practice of law. He moved to Elizabeth in 1869 and died there on June 9, 1872. He is buried in Saint Mary's Episcopal Churchyard in Burlington. (Gillette, *Jersey Blue*; Lurie, *A New Jersey Anthology*)

Joseph G. Bilby

Marcus Lawrence Ward was born in Newark to a prominent family on November 9, 1812. Ward became a leading businessman in the city and a director of the National State Bank. He was also a well-known and idealistic philanthropist who contributed both time and money to worthy causes, including public libraries and the New Jersey Historical Society. In the pre-war period, Ward became a leading figure in the New Jersey Republican Party as well.

With the outbreak of war, Ward established an office in Newark for the purpose of aiding New Jersey's soldiers at the front and their families at home. He threw himself into the cause wholeheartedly, as his voluminous correspondence from the era, now held by the

Marcus Lawrence Ward (John W. Kuhl)

New Jersey Historical Society, attests. Ward sent aid to hospitals in the field and also established the Soldiers' Home in Newark as a haven for wounded veterans. These contributions and services won him the well earned nickname "the soldiers' friend," and Ward General Hospital in Newark was named for him. Ward ran for governor as a Republican in 1862, but was overwhelmingly defeated by Democrat **Joel Parker**.

In 1865, Ward ran once more for governor, was elected and served from 1866 to 1869. Initially ambivalent, his administration came down on the side of Congressional Reconstruction and against President Andrew Johnson's lenient policy towards ex-Confederate leaders. Ward's leadership helped to insure approval of the Fourteenth Amendment by the New Jersey legislature, but subsequent Republican electoral defeats in the state led him to moderate support for extending African-American male suffrage. Otherwise his record was substantially progressive, and his administration mandated public education, among other accomplishments.

Ward subsequently served one term in the Congress as a representative from New Jersey, from 1873 to 1875. In 1884, he caught malaria while visiting Florida and died at home on April 25, 1884. He was buried in Mount Pleasant Cemetery in Newark. (Gillette, *Jersey Blue*; Lurie & Mappen, *Encyclopedia of New Jersey*; Stellhorn & Birkner, *The Governors of New Jersey*)

Dr. David G. Martin

Timothy Webster was born in Newhaven, England on March 12, 1822, immigrated to America at age eight, and settled with his parents in Princeton, New Jersey. In 1841, Webster married a local girl and became a successful machinist. Seeking a more challenging and interesting career, however, he left Princeton in 1853 to become a policeman at New York's Crystal Palace Exposition. While in New York, Webster met Allan Pinkerton and joined that famous detective's organization. Within a few years he was acknowledged as one of Pinkerton's best agents.

Timothy Webster (*Harper's Magazine*)

When the Civil War began, Webster's pre-war experience as an undercover agent served him well. He had befriended many secessionists and even infiltrated the Knights of Liberty, a secret organization of secession sympathizers. Webster was credited by Pinkerton with discovering and foiling the plot to assassinate Abraham Lincoln in Baltimore as the president-elect passed through the city on his way to his first inauguration. Webster later became a messenger for the *Richmond Examiner*, a position that allowed him ready access to Confederate military and industrial sites. His intelligence reports on blockade runners led to the seizure of many shipments of war material to the Confederacy.

In 1862, Webster developed a case of rheumatism attributed to exposure during his duties. Two men sent to replace him were recognized as federal spies and, arrested and interrogated, revealed information that led to Webster's apprehension. While the informers were eventually released, Webster was found guilty of spying and sentenced to be hanged despite his request for a firing squad. After a hooded Webster mounted the gallows in Richmond on April 29, 1862, the noose around his neck slipped off when the trapdoor sprung. Webster fell to the ground, was assisted back up the steps, and the rope was again looped over his head. As he exclaimed, "I suffer a double death," the trap was again released and he dropped to his doom, the first American hanged as a spy since Nathan Hale. The Webster family suffered another tragic loss to the war when his son, Timothy Jr., wounded at the battle of Brice's Crossroads, Mississippi, died in 1864 of the effects of a leg amputation while a prisoner of the Rebels in Mobile, Alabama. (Sifakis, *Who Was Who*)

John W. Kuhl

Walt Whitman is one of America's best-known poets. Born near Huntington, Long Island, on May 31, 1819, Whitman moved with his family to Brooklyn as a child. He was trained as a printer and became a journalist as well, and in 1846 became editor of the *Brooklyn Eagle*, a position from which he was subsequently fired for his abolitionist beliefs. After leaving the *Eagle*, Whitman took up poetry. He published the first edition of his noted work *Leaves of Grass* in 1855 and spent the rest of his life revising it. The book was not critically well received initially, as the critics of the day were not used to free verse, but other writers and poets quickly recognized Whitman's genius. A prototype of the 1950s "Beat Generation" poet, Whitman settled in with writers and artists of similar spirit in lower Manhattan in the late 1850s.

Walt Whitman (Library of Congress)

The Civil War had a great impact on Whitman, both personally and artistically. When his brother George was wounded at the battle of Fredericksburg in December 1862, Whitman went to Washington to care for him in a hospital there. The poet was so stricken by the suffering he saw that he stayed on to serve as a male nurse for the remainder of the war. Whitman's strong feelings about the war were expressed in his book *Drum Taps* (1865), which includes his famous poem inspired by the death of President Lincoln, "O Captain! My Captain!"

In the postwar era, Whitman's literary genius finally began to be recognized, and he was able to make a living as a writer and speaker. He moved to Camden, New Jersey, in 1873 "by accident" and found a home there for the rest of his life. Walt Whitman died in Camden on March 26, 1892. He is buried in the city's Harleigh Cemetery in a self-designed mausoleum. His Camden home is preserved as a state historic site. Otherwise, the public is reminded of his greatness in classic New Jersey fashion – as a bridge and a turnpike rest area.
(*http://www.ci.camden.nj.us/attractions/waltwhitman.html*; Lurie & Mappen, *Encyclopedia of New Jersey*)

Dr. David G. Martin

Alfred Alexander Woodhull was born in Princeton, New Jersey, on April 13, 1837, to Alfred and Anna Maria Salomon Woodhull. Woodhull, a descendant of Declaration of Independence signer John Witherspoon, received his B.A and M.A. degrees from Princeton and then his M.D. from the University of Pennsylvania. After graduation, he moved to Kansas and practiced there for two years.

At the outset of the Civil War, Woodhull was commissioned a lieutenant in a Kansas militia unit. In September 1861, he was appointed to the U. S. Army Volunteer Medical Corps and in 1864 became medical inspector of the Army of the James. In Washington at the close of the war, he treated Secretary of State William H. Seward after Seward was stabbed by John Wilkes Booth assassination co-conspirator Lewis Powell. After the war, Woodhull remained in the army and prepared the surgical section of the *Catalogue of the US Army Medical Museum*. In 1868, he married Margaret Ellicott of Baltimore. The couple had no children. Doctor Woodhull specialized in military hygiene and public health issues and became an instructor in military hygiene at Fort Leavenworth, then commanding officer and medical director of several military hospitals, and was appointed Chief Surgeon, Department of the Pacific, serving in the Philippines for six months in 1899.

**Alfred Alexander Woodhull
(U. S. Army Medical Corps)**

Expanding on his interest in hygiene, Woodhull became a leading expert on tropical diseases and their transmission, given the knowledge base of the era. He authored numerous military and medical publications, including *Military Hygiene for Officers of the Line*, which remained the U.S. Military Academy's principal reference text on the subject until 1914. Although the mosquito had yet to be identified as a yellow-fever vector, Woodhull's article on the etiology of an 1876 Savannah outbreak considered germ theory as a hypothesis and concluded the epidemic had a local rather than foreign origin. Woodhull's strong views that sanitation was essential for preventing the spread of disease and that preventing disease was a critical element in maintaining military effectiveness were vindicated during the Spanish-American War, when typhoid proved the major killer of American soldiers.

Woodhull retired from the army in 1901 as a brigadier general and returned to New Jersey, where he lectured on general sanitation and hygiene at Princeton University from 1902 to 1907 He died on October 18, 1921, and is buried in Princeton Cemetery. (Cirillo, "Fever and Reform"; Lurie & Mappen, *Encyclopedia of New Jersey*)

Valerie M. Josephson

Percy Wyndham was born on September 22, 1833, aboard his father's ship, then floating off the British coast. Seeking a life of adventure, Wyndham fought in the French Revolution of 1848 and later served as an ensign in the French navy. He subsequently returned to England for a stint in the British army, then left to serve as a squadron commander in the Austrian cavalry. In 1860, Wyndham forsook the Austrians to fight under Giuseppe Garibaldi in Italy, earning the Military Order of Savoy from King Victor Emmanuel, which enabled him to style himself "Sir Percy" ever after. Wyndham admired the American concept of liberty and in 1861 crossed the ocean to fight against slavery and, incidentally, win fame and glory.

Percy Wyndham (USAMHI/MOLLUS)

Governor **Charles Olden** chose Wyndham to replace the inept Colonel William Halsted of the 1st New Jersey Cavalry, and aided by Lieutenant Colonel **Joseph Kargé** , he quickly whipped the regiment into shape. An impetuous commander, Wyndham was unhorsed and captured in an ambush near Harrisonburg, Virginia, in May 1862. Exchanged two months later, he was back in the saddle again at Second Bull Run, where one Jersey trooper noted that the hotter the action became, the more vigorously the colonel twirled his moustache, easily the most distinctive facial hair of the war.

In late 1862, Colonel Wyndham became a brigade commander, and pursued famed Confederate partisan John S. Mosby with no result save the loss of two uniforms to the Rebel raider. He redeemed himself with a stellar performance at Brandy Station in June 1863, however, where he conducted a brilliant rear-guard action and was wounded in the leg. Wyndham convalesced on light duty in Washington until mustered out in July 1864.

After leaving the army, Wyndham ran a military school in New York and then became part owner of a petroleum refinery, which unfortunately exploded. Moving on to India, he established a Calcutta newspaper and then dissipated its profits in a failed Burmese logging venture. Broke and down on his luck, in January 1879 Wyndham built a huge rag-tag balloon, charging spectators to watch him ascend over a Rangoon lake. The balloon, and the colonel, exploded in mid-air, ending the colorful career of perhaps the most eccentric nineteenth-century honorary New Jerseyan. (Longacre, *Jersey Cavaliers*; Toombs, *New Jersey Troops in the Gettysburg Campaign*)

Joseph G. Bilby

Abram Zabriskie was born on February 18, 1841, in Hackensack, third son of well-known New Jersey attorney A. O. Zabriskie. Following his mother's death, the family moved to Jersey City, where he attended Edgehill Preparatory School. He graduated from Princeton University in 1859, then studied law. Zabriskie gained a reputation for selfless courage early on, when at the age of nineteen he aided in the heroic rescue of his sister and a fisherman caught in a fierce ocean eddy at Long Branch.

Abram Zabriskie (Greg Speciale)

In October 1861, Zabriskie abandoned plans for a European tour and enlisted in the 9th New Jersey Infantry as a lieutenant. He was appointed regimental adjutant, an important junior-officer position in a regiment, managing the unit's paperwork. The 9th, a regiment of marksmen, counted Newark German target shooters and Ocean County duck hunters in its ranks, and was selected to participate in General Ambrose Burnside's 1862 North Carolina expedition by sea. While landing at Cape Hatteras on January 15, a surfboat conveying the 9th's headquarters detachment, Colonel Joseph Allen, Lieutenant Colonel Charles Heckman, Surgeon Frederick Weller and Zabriskie, overturned in rough water and the colonel and surgeon drowned. As a result, Heckman was promoted to colonel and Zabriskie was elevated to lieutenant colonel.

The 9th was engaged at Roanoke Island in February 1862, and went on to fight at New Bern and other actions in North Carolina. A talented officer, Zabriskie was promoted to colonel in January 1863. In the spring of 1864, the regiment was reassigned to the Virginia theater and joined the advance of General Benjamin Butler's army on Richmond. The 9th was protecting the Union right flank at Drewry's Bluff on May 16 when the Confederates counterattacked. The regiment sacrificed itself in a rear-guard action that saved the army, but Colonel Zabriskie was shot in the throat with a bullet that lodged near his spine. He stayed on his feet, rallying his men, until he collapsed from loss of blood and was taken from the field.

Evacuated to Chesapeake Army Hospital, Zabriskie lingered, deliriously muttering "Poor boys, poor boys; they are in a bad scrape" over and over until his death on May 24. His body was returned to Jersey City for a well-attended funeral service at the First Dutch Reformed Church. He was buried at Green-Wood Cemetery in Brooklyn. (Bilby & Goble, *Remember You Are Jerseymen*; Drake, *History of the Ninth*)

Sylvia Mogerman

The Contributors

Henry F. Ballone is retired as owner and operator of a firm making film for printers and is currently a photojournalist and graphic designer. He is a member of the New Jersey Civil War Heritage Association and its 150th Anniversary Committee, as well as the Board of Advisors of the Lincoln Forum, the Executive Committee of The Lincoln Group of New York, the Executive Board of The Phil Kearny Civil War Round Table and other Lincoln and Civil War organizations. He is the graphic designer of The Lincoln Group of New York "Wide Awake" bulletin, The Lincoln Forum "Bulletin," and several books, including this one. His Lincoln and Civil War event photos are posted at: web.me.com/civilwarnut

Joseph G. Bilby received his BA and MA degrees in history from Seton Hall University, served as an army officer in the Vietnam War and is the author of a number of books on New Jersey and military history, including *Remember You Are Jerseymen* with William Goble. Retired from the New Jersey Department of Labor as Supervising Investigator, he is a trustee of the New Jersey Civil War Heritage Association, website content editor for it's 150th Anniversary Committee and assistant curator of the National Guard Militia Museum of New Jersey in Sea Girt.

Thomas R. Burke, Jr. is a trustee of the New Jersey Civil War Heritage Association and member of its 150th Anniversary Committee. He has been active in the Civil War reenacting community for many years and is currently a member of the Winfield Scott Hancock Society, the 69th NYSVHA, the 6th New York Independent Battery and the 13th NJVI. He has been published in *Civil War Historian* magazine and contributed to National Park Service documentary projects.

Catherine Cassidy of Wood-Ridge, New Jersey, has been a history teacher for sixteen years. She is co-author of the Arcadia Press "Images of America" series book, *Wood-Ridge,* and author of the series' *Hasbrouck Heights* title. She serves on a number of historical association boards, has a deep interest in New Jersey state and local history and is an avid Civil War buff.

Norman A. Dykstra had his childhood interest in the Civil War renewed during a 1993 visit to New Orleans' Confederate Memorial Hall Museum. He is a charter member and secretary of the New Jersey Civil War Heritage Association, a member of the Phil Kearny Civil War Round Table and a life member of the Iron Brigade Association.

Bruce M. Form received a BA in history from Athens State University and an MA in behavioral science from Kean University. He is a retired Woodbridge Township high school vice principal, member of the executive committee of the Robert E. Lee Civil War Round Table and executive director of the Round Table's Civil War Library and Research Center. Mr. Form and his wife, Mira Katz Form, are students of the role of Jews in the Civil War, and he portrays Captain Myer Asch in living history presentations.

Thomas Fox is retired from a long and successful career as basketball coach of Pope John XXIII high school in Sparta, New Jersey, and is currently a school librarian. He is the author of *Drummer Boy Willie Mcgee.*

Steven D. Glazer received his BA, BSEE and JD degrees from Rutgers University, and an MS from Fairleigh Dickinson University. Mr. Glazer retired as a lieutenant colonel in the USAR in 1997, after serving six years as an intelligence/electronic-warfare officer in the Pentagon. He is a partner of the law firm of Weil, Gotshal & Manges LLP and adjunct professor of law at Rutgers.

John Hallanan received his BA in history from Rutgers University and is retired from a career in information technology. He served 28 years in the National Guard, mostly in the 69th New York of Civil War fame, before retiring as a Sergeant E-7, and is currently Junior Vice Commander of the 69th's Veteran Corps. He is past president and current treasurer of the Lincoln Association of Jersey City, a Division Historian of the Ancient Order of Hibernians and a member of numerous other organizations.

Valerie M. Josephson received her BA degree from George Washington University and edited a medical journal for many years. Her great-grandfather was seriously wounded during the Civil War, spurring her interest in Civil War medicine. She is currently writing a book on the nine surgeons of the four New Jersey militia regiments.

John W. Kuhl is a graduate of Penn State University who spent three years as a U.S. Navy deck officer and navigator in the Antarctic during the 1950s. A lifelong student and leading collector of New Jersey related Civil War relics and photographs and author of articles on the state's soldiers, he is retired from an agricultural career in his native Hunterdon County.

Robert F. MacAvoy, a USAF Vietnam veteran, retired in 2002 as a senior supervisor/project engineer for Merck & Co., Rahway. He is co-author, with Charles Eckhardt, of *Our Brothers Gone Before*, an inventory of Civil War burials in New Jersey cemeteries, and is currently searching for the names of over 10,000 Civil War veterans who may also be buried in New Jersey cemeteries in addition to the 41,000 already found, as well as out of state burials of veterans with ties to New Jersey.

James M. Madden received his BA in marketing from Saint Peter's College and has contributed articles to many Civil War publications and projects. A political consultant, he is also a trustee of the New Jersey Civil War Heritage Association, a member of its 150th Anniversary Committee and a trustee of the Historic Jersey City And Harsimus Cemetery.

David G. Martin received his BA from the University of Michigan and holds MA and PhD degrees from Princeton University. He is a teacher and administrator at the Peddie School, president of the New Jersey Civil War Heritage Association, and publisher/editor of Longstreet House book company. Dr. Martin is author and editor of a number of works on the Civil War, including *Gettysburg July 1* and *Jackson's Valley Campaign*, and on New Jersey's role in the war, including *The Monocacy Regiment.*

Rich Mendoza received his BA from Glassboro State College and is a member of the New Jersey Civil War Heritage Association and its 150th Anniversary Committee, as well as captain of the 12th New Jersey Volunteer Infantry Company "K" reenacting unit. A retired teacher, he now works in television and as a songwriter. He has produced Civil War music videos and worked on a number of Civil War films, including *Glory* and *Gettysburg*, and makes presentations at schools and Civil War roundtables.

Sylvia Mogerman has a BA in elementary and secondary English education and was a teacher for over thirty years. She is now editor, publicist and board member of the Phil Kearny Civil War Round Table, board member and historian for the League of Historical Societies of New Jersey, a member of the New Jersey Civil War Heritage Association's 150th Anniversary Committee and a volunteer for Golden Retriever Rescue of New Jersey.

Fr. David G. Moreno, SDB, earned a BD in theology from St. Patrick's College, Maynooth, Ireland, and an MA in history from Fordham University. He is currently Dean of Studies at the Salesian seminary residence in Orange, New Jersey. Fr. Moreno is an active Civil War reenactor, serving as Chaplain of the 7th New Jersey Volunteer Infantry.

Pamela Newhouse received a BA in advertising design from the University of Michigan and an MA in historic preservation from Eastern Michigan University. She was a National Park Service seasonal historian and Gettysburg Summer Scholar award winner. Co-founder and former vice president and program chairperson of the Ann Arbor Civil War Round Table, she is editor of "The Sultana Remembered" newsletter and has appeared on the History Channel.

Diana Newman holds BS degrees in music and nursing and an MA in film & broadcasting. She has taught in New York and Ohio, where she received national recognition for developing an educational program. As a former member of the 5th Ohio Light Artillery and 6th New York Independent Battery Light Artillery, she represented women who, disguised as men, fought as Civil War soldiers. She is a member of the Camp Olden Civil War Roundtable, a volunteer at the National Guard Militia Museum of New Jersey in Sea Girt and, with Robert Silverman, presents Civil War living history programs to organizations in New Jersey.

Bernard A. Olsen received his BS and MAT degrees from Monmouth University and is the author of two New Jersey related Civil War books, *Upon The Tented Field* and *A Billy Yank Governor: The Life & Times of New Jersey's Franklin Murphy*. He is a retired high school history teacher and has served as an adjunct instructor at Georgian Court University and Brookdale Community College.

Robert Silverman received his BS in aerospace engineering and MS in mechanical engineering from Syracuse University. After serving as an army officer, he pursued a career as a research engineer, receiving three US patents. He is a former member of the 5th Ohio Light Artillery and 6th New York Independent Battery Light Artillery, a member of the Camp Olden Civil War Roundtable, a volunteer at the National Guard Militia Museum of New Jersey in Sea Girt and, with Diana Newman, presents Civil War living history programs to organizations in New Jersey.

William B. Styple is a graduate of Catawba College. He has authored, co-authored and edited a number of works on the Civil War, several with New Jersey significance, including *The Civil War Letters of General Philip Kearny* and *The Andersonville Memoirs of Charles Hopkins*.

Lesley-Ann Thomson received her BA in American history/secondary education from Ramapo College of New Jersey and is currently completing her MA in American history at Monmouth University. She teaches US and New Jersey history at Barnegat High School, is a member of the New Jersey Civil War 150th Anniversary Committee and recently received the Patriot's Podium Award for a lecture on New Jersey's Role in the American Revolution.

Joseph A. Truglio is a retired motion picture film technician and lifelong student of the American Civil War. He is a member of the New Jersey Civil War Heritage Association's 150th Anniversary Committee as well as several Civil War round tables and is currently president of the Phil Kearny Civil War Round Table in Wayne.

Jason Wickersty received his BA in history from Montclair State University and teaches social studies at Christa McAuliffe Middle School in Jackson, New Jersey. He is also a National Park Service Ranger with the National Park Education Center of New York Harbor at Fort Wadsworth, a member of the Center for Civil War Photography and Civil War Preservation Trust, and has been published in "Hallowed Ground," the Trust's official magazine.

John Zinn received BA and MBA degrees from Rutgers University and served as an army officer in the Vietnam War. He is currently the chairman of the 150th Anniversary Committee and the chairman of the board of the New Jersey Historical Society. He is the author of the *The Mutinous Regiment: The Thirty-third New Jersey in the Civil War* and *The Major League Pennant Races of 1916: The Most Maddening Baseball Melee in History* (with Paul Zinn).

Selected Bibliography

Includes fuller citations for further sources on individual biographies

Books

Allerdice, Bruce S. *More Generals in Gray.* Baton Rouge: LSU Press, 1995.

Barnett, Louise K. *Ungentlemanly Acts: The Army's Notorious Incest Trial.* New York: Hill and Wang, 2001.

Bayard, Samuel J. *The Life of George Dashiell Bayard Late Captain, U. S. A. and Brigadier General of Volunteers, Killed at the Battle of Fredericksburg.* New York: G. P. Putnam's Sons, 1874.

Bazelon, Bruce and William McGuinn. *Directory of American Military Goods Dealers and Makers, 1785-1915.* Manassas, VA: Authors, 1999.

Bellard, Alfred. (David Herbert Donald ed.) *Gone for a Soldier: The Civil War Memoirs of Private Alfred Bellard.* Boston: Little Brown & Company, 1975.

Bethel, Elizabeth Rauh. *The Roots of African-American Identity.* New York: Palgrave Macmillan, 1997.

Bilby, Joseph G. *Three Rousing Cheers: A History of the Fifteenth New Jersey Infantry from Flemington to Appomattox.* Hightstown, NJ: Longstreet House, 1993. (2001 edition)

_____. *Forgotten Warriors: New Jersey's African American Soldiers in the Civil War.* Hightstown, NJ: Longstreet House, 1993.

_____. *Remember Fontenoy: The 69th New York and the Irish Brigade in the Civil War.* Hightstown, NJ: Longstreet House, 1995. (1997 edition)

_____. and William C. Goble. *"Remember You Are Jerseymen": A Military History of New Jersey's Troops in the Civil War.* Hightstown, NJ: Longstreet House, 1998.

_____. *Sea Girt: A Brief History.* Charleston, SC: The History Press, 2008.

_____. and Harry Ziegler. *Asbury Park: A Brief History.* Charleston, SC: The History Press, 2009.

Bishop, John Leander, Edwin Troxell Freedley and Edward Young. *A History of American Manufactures from 1608 to 1860.* New York: E. D. Young, 1868.

Blanton, Deanne and Lauren M. Cook. *They Fought Like Demons: Women Soldiers in the Civil War.* Baton Rouge: LSU Press, 2002.

Brockett, Linus P. and Mary C. Vaughn. *Women's Work in the Civil War: A Record of Heroism, Patriotism and Patience*. Philadelphia: Zeigler McCurdy & Co., 1867.

Bruce, Robert V. *Lincoln and the Tools of War*. Chicago: University of Chicago Press, 1989.

Cogar, William B. *Dictionary of Admirals of the U. S. Navy, 1862-1900*. Washington: Naval Institute Press, 1989.

Crowell, Joseph E. *The Young Volunteer: A Record of the Experiences of a Private Soldier Boy in the Civil War*. London and New York: F. Tennyson Neely, 1899.

Cumming, John. *Runners and Walkers: A Nineteenth Century Sports Chronicle*. Chicago: Regnery Gateway, 1981.

Detzer, David. *Allegiance: Fort Sumter, Charleston, and the Beginning of the Civil War*. New York: Harcourt, 2001.

Drake, J. Madison. *The History of the Ninth New Jersey Veteran Volunteers*. Elizabeth, NJ: Journal Printing House, 1889.

Eckhardt, Charles and Robert MacAvoy. *Our Brothers Gone Before* (2 Vols). Hightstown, NJ: Longstreet House, 2006.

Eicher, John H. and David J. Eicher. *Civil War High Commands*. Stanford: Stanford University Press, 2001.

Faust, Drew Gilpin. *This Republic of Suffering: Death and the American Civil War*. New York: Alfred A Knopf, 2008.

Fishel, Edwin C. *The Secret War for the Union: The Untold Story of Military Intelligence in the Civil War*. New York: Houghton Mifflin, 1996.

Ford, William F. *The Industrial Interests of Newark, N.J., Containing an Historical Sketch of the City, also a Complete Summary of the Origin, Growth and Present Condition of Newark's Industries, Including the Location and Description of all the Manufacturing Establishments*. New York: Van Arsdale & Company, 1874.

Foster, John Y. *New Jersey and the Rebellion: A History of the Services of the Troops and People of New Jersey in Aid of the Union Cause*. Newark: Dennis & Company, 1868.

Fox, Thomas. *Drummer Boy Willie McGee, Civil War Hero and Fraud*. Jefferson, NC: McFarland Publishing, 2008.

Francine, Albert P. *Louis Raymond Francine, Brevet Brigadier-General, U.S. Volunteers*. Hightstown, NJ: Longstreet House, 2000.

French, Samuel. *Two Wars: An Autobiography*. Nashville, TN: Confederate Veteran, 1901.

Gillette, William. *Jersey Blue: Civil War Politics in New Jersey, 1854-1865*. New Brunswick, NJ: Rutgers University Press, 1994.

Haines, Alanson. *History of the Fifteenth Regiment New Jersey Volunteers*. New York: Jenkins & Thomas, 1883.

Haines, William P. *History of the Men of Co. F, with Description of the Marches and Battles of the 12th New Jersey Vols*. Woodbury, NJ: Gloucester County Historical Society. (Reprint of 1897 edition)

Heroux, Jennifer and Stuart C. Mobray. *Civil War Arms Makers and their Contracts: A Facsimile Reprint of the Report by the Commission on Ordnance and Ordnance Stores, 1862*. Lincoln, RI: Andrew Mobray, 1998.

Herringshaw, Thomas William. *Herringshaw's National Library of American Biography*. Chicago: American Publishers' Assn., 1909.

Holzer, Harold, and Mark E. Neely, Jr. *Mine Eyes Have Seen the Glory: The Civil War in Art*. New York: Orion Books, 1993.

Johnson, Rossiter, ed. *The Twentieth Century Biographical Dictionary of Notable Americans*, Boston: The Biographical Society, 1904.

Kajencki, Francis C. *Star on Many a Battlefield: Brevet Brigadier General Joseph Kargé in the American Civil War*. Rutherford, NJ: Fairleigh Dickinson University Press, 1980.

Luzky, Colonel (ret.) Leonard, ed. *The Adjutants General of New Jersey, 1776-2002*. Lawrenceville, NJ: NJDMAVA, 2003.

Larson, R.D. *White Roses: Stories of Civil War Nurses*. Gettysburg, PA: Thomas Publications, 1997.

Longacre, Edward G. *To Gettysburg and Beyond: The Twelfth New Jersey Volunteer Infantry, II Corps, Army of the Potomac, 1862-1865*. Hightstown, NJ: Longstreet House, 1988.

_____. *Jersey Cavaliers: A History of the First New Jersey Volunteer Cavalry, 1861-1865*. Hightstown, NJ: Longstreet House, 1992.

Lurie, Maxine N., ed. *A New Jersey Anthology*. New Brunswick, NJ: Rutgers University Press, 1994.

_____ and Marc Mappen. *Encyclopedia of New Jersey*. New Brunswick, NJ: Rutgers University Press, 2004.

McCullough, David. *The Great Bridge*. New York: Simon & Schuster, 1972.

McPhee, John. *The Deltoid Pumpkin Seed*. New York: Farrar, Straus & Giroux, 1992

Mappen, Marc. *Jerseyana: The Underside of New Jersey History*. New Brunswick, NJ: Rutgers University Press, 1992.

Marquis, Albert Nelson. *Who's Who In America, 1908-1909: A Biographical Dictionary of Notable Living Men and Women in the United States*. Chicago: Marquis Publishing, 1909.

Martin, Dr. David G., ed. *The Monocacy Regiment: A Commemorative History of the Fourteenth New Jersey Infantry in the Civil War, 1862-1865*. Hightstown, NJ: Longstreet House, 1987.

Martin, Samuel J. *Kill-Cavalry, Sherman's Merchant of Terror: The Life of Union General Hugh Judson Kilpatrick*. Teaneck, NJ: Fairleigh Dickinson University Press, 1996.

Merrill, James. *DuPont, The Making of an Admiral*. New York: Dodd, Mead, 1986.

Miers, Earl Schenck. *Where the Raritan Flows*. New Brunswick, NJ: Rutgers University Press, 1964.

_____. *New Jersey and the Civil War*. Princeton: D. Van Nostrand Co., 1964.

Mitros, David. *Gone to Wear the Victor's Crown: Morris County, New Jersey and the Civil War – A Documentary Account*. Morristown: Morris County Historical Commission, 1998.

Nichols, James Moses and James Verner Scaife. *Perry's Saints: Or, The Fighting Parson's Regiment in the War of the Rebellion: History of the 48th NY*. New York: D. Lothrop, 1886.

Olsen, Bernard. *A Billy Yank Governor: The Life and Times of New Jersey's Franklin Murphy*. West Kennebunk, ME: Phoenix Publishing, 2000.

Paine, Albert Bigelow. *Thomas Nast: His Period and Pictures*. New York: MacMillan Company, 1904.

Peterson, Harold. *The American Sword, 1775-1943*. Philadelphia: Ray Riling, 1973 (Revised edition)

Raum, John O. *History of the City of Trenton, New Jersey: Embracing a Period of Nearly Two Hundred Years, Commencing in 1676, the First Settlement of the Town, and Extending Up to the Present Time, with Official Records of the Population, Extent of the Town at Different Periods, Its Manufactories, Church ...* Trenton: W. T. Nicholson, 1871.

Reeds, Karen. *A State of Health: New Jersey's Medical Heritage*. New Brunswick, NJ: Rutgers University Press, 2001.

Revere, Joseph W. *Keel and Saddle: A Retrospect of Forty Years of Naval and Military Service.* Boston: Osgood and Company, 1872.

Rhea, Gordon. *The Battles for Spotsylvania Court House.* Baton Rouge: LSU Press, 1997.

Robertson, James I., ed. *The Civil War Letters of Robert McAllister.* New Brunswick, NJ: Rutgers University Press, 1965.

Rogers, Grace Norton, Maurice P. Shuman and Dr. David G. Martin. *Clara Barton and Hightstown.* Hightstown, NJ: Longstreet House, 1994.

Sackett, William Edgar. *Modern Battles of Trenton: Being a History of New Jersey's Politics and Legislation from the Year 1868 to the Year 1894.* Trenton: John L. Murray, 1895.

Saretzky, Gary D. and Eugene Osovitz. *The Civil War and Monmouth County: An Exhibition at the Monmouth County Library Headquarters.* Manalapan, NJ: Monmouth County Archives, 2006.

Sears, Stephen W. *George B. McClellan: The Young Napoleon.* New York: Da Capo Press, 1999.

Schwartz, Cipora O. *An American Jewish Odyssey: American Religious Freedom and the Nathan Barnert Memorial Temple.* Franklin Lakes, NJ: Congregation B'nai Jeshrurum, 2008.

Scott, Donald Sr. *Camp William Penn.* Charleston, SC: Arcadia, 2008.

Sellers, Frank M. *Sharps Firearms.* Alstead, NH: Sellers Publishing, 1988.

Siegel, Alan A. *For the Glory of the Union: Myth, Reality and the Media in Civil War New Jersey.* Teaneck, NJ: Fairleigh Dickinson University Press, 1984.

Sifakis, Stewart. *Who Was Who in the Civil War.* New York: Facts on File, 1989.

Stellhorn, Paul A. and Michael J. Birkner. *The Governors of New Jersey, 1664-1974.* Trenton: New Jersey Historical Commission, 1982.

Still, William. *The Underground Railroad: A Record of Facts, Authentic Narratives, Letters, Etc.* Philadelphia: Porter and Coates, 1872.

Styple, William B., ed. *The Civil War Letters of General Philip Kearny.* Kearny, NJ: Belle Grove Publishing, 1988.

_____ and John J. Fitzpatrick, ed. *The Andersonville Diary and Memoirs of Charles Hopkins, 1st New Jersey Infantry.* Kearny, NJ: Belle Grove Publishing, 1988.

Switala, William J. *Underground Railroad in New York and New Jersey*. New York: Stackpole, 2006.

The Biographical Encyclopedia of New Jersey of the 19th Century. Philadelphia: Galaxy Publishing, 1877.

Toombs, Samuel. *New Jersey Troops in the Gettysburg Campaign*. Hightstown, NJ: Longstreet House, 1992. (Reprint of 1888 edition)

Tuttle, Brad R. *How Newark Became Newark: The Rise, Fall and Rebirth of an American City*. New Brunswick, NJ: Rutgers University Press, 2009.

Urquhart, Frank J. *A Short History of Newark* Newark: Baker Printing, 1953. (Public school edition)

Warner, Ezra J. *Generals in Blue: Lives of the Union Commanders*. Baton Rouge: LSU Press, 1964. (1994 edition)

Welch, Richard F. *The Boy General: The Life and Careers of Francis Channing Barlow*. Kent, OH: Kent State University Press, 2003.

Welling, William. *Photography in the Americas, the Formative Years 1829-1900*. Albuquerque: University of New Mexico Press, 1987.

Zinn, John. *The Mutinous Regiment: The Thirty-third New Jersey in the Civil War*. Jefferson, NC: McFarland & Co., 2005.

Articles

Bilby, Joseph G. "Colonel Myron Beaumont, 1st New Jersey Cavalry." *Military Images Magazine*, July-August 1989.

_____. "Through Hades with his Hat Off: The Strange Career of A. J. Morrison." *Military Images Magazine*, March-April 1990.

_____. "An Officer and a Gentleman...Sort Of." *Military Images Magazine*, January-February 1992.

_____. "Timothy Shaw, 43rd U.S. Colored Infantry." *Military Images Magazine*, May-June 1993.

Cirillo, Vincent J. "Fever and Reform: The Typhoid Epidemic in the Spanish-American War." *Journal of Historical Medicine and Allied Sciences* 55(4) 2000.

Cleveland, Edmund J. Jr. ed. "Early Campaigns in North Carolina: The Diary of Private Edmund J. Cleveland, Company L, 9th New Jersey Volunteers." *New Jersey Historical Society Proceedings*, Vol. 66 (1948) through Vol. 71 (1953) serially.

Colie, Edward M. "Cortland Parker, 1818-1907," *Proceedings of the New Jersey Historical Society*, April 1920.

Kuhl, John W. "General George W. Taylor: Hunterdon County's Only Civil War General." *Hunterdon Historical Newsletter*, Winter 1980.

Loewan, Susan Irish. "The Captain and Mrs. Irish." *The Castle Genie: Newsletter of the Passaic County Historical Society Genealogy Club*, Vol. 10, No. 1 (2000).

McAfee, Michael J. "20th New York Volunteer Infantry, the United Turner Rifles." *Military Images Magazine*, May-June 1999.

Madden, James M. & Ronald P. McGovern. "A Wedding in Camp." *Blue & Gray Magazine*, February 1992.

Miller, Guy. "Recollections of Hambletonian 10." *Harness Horse*, December 10, 1948.

Newhouse, Pamela. "Chester Berry: 'Sweet Hour of Prayer.'" *The Sultana Remembered*, Spring 2005.

"Obituary of Charles Deshler." *Proceedings and Papers Read Before the Lehigh County Historical Society*, Volume II (1910).

Ragan, Mark K. "A Union Whale Surfaces in New Jersey." *America's Civil War*, May, 2008.

Newspapers

Jersey City *American Standard*

Newark Daily Advertiser

Newark Evening News

New York Times

Red Bank Register

Trenton *True American*

Trenton *Gazette*

West Paterson *Herald News*

Manuscripts

Archives of the Episcopal Diocese of New Jersey

Rosé papers

Morris County Historical Society

Alexander Vandoni diary

New Jersey Historical Society

Josiah Brown, "Civil War Reminiscences, 1861-65,"

Horace N. Congar papers

Edward A. Pierson papers

Rutgers University Library Special Collections

J. Toffey papers.

US Army Military History Institute

Edmund Halsey journal.

Other

Turvey, John. Powerpoint presentation on the life of Isaac Gordon to Madison NJ Historical Society

Zinn, John. "Team History of the Eureka Base Ball Club of Newark." (unpublished manuscript)

Biographies of 150 New Jerseyans Caught Up in the Struggle of the Civil War

Index